Strength in Adversity:
A Study of the Alberta Economy

Publication No. 1 in
Western Studies in Economic Policy,
a joint series of the
Western Centre for Economic Research
at the University of Alberta
and the
C. D. Howe Institute

Robert L. Mansell

&

Michael B. Percy

Published by the

University of Alberta Press

First published by The University of Alberta Press
141 Athabasca Hall, Edmonton, Alberta, Canada
T6G 2E8
Copyright © The University of Alberta Press 1990

Canadian Cataloguing in Publication Data
Mansell, Robert L.
  Strength in adversity

  (Western studies in economic policy ; no. 1)
  Includes bibliographical references.
  ISBN 0-88864-232-6

  1. Alberta – Economic conditions – 1945-*
2. Alberta – Economic policy. I. Percy, Michael,
1948- II. C.D. Howe Institute.   III. Title.
IV. Series.
HC117.A4M36 1990   330.97123'03   C90-091698-2

Published in conjunction with the C.D. Howe Institute.

Printed by Printing Services, The University of Alberta
Edmonton, Alberta, Canada

Contents

Figures

T ables

Appendix Tables

Preface

With publication of this study, the C.D. Howe Institute and the Western
Centre for Economic Research at the University of Alberta commence a joint
venture in a new series, *Western Studies in Economic Policy. Strength in
Adversity* by Robert Mansell and Michael Percy of the Universities of Calgary
and Alberta respectively, focuses on Alberta's problems of instability,
particularly during the 1980s. The authors find that regardless of the measure
of instability chosen, the Alberta economy ranked among the most unstable in
Canada and comparable American states over the period 1961-85. Their
detailed analysis of the Alberta economy in the 1980s shows that, while many
seeds of the sharp drop in economic activity in Alberta in 1982-83 were sown
in the 1970s by predictable market forces and consequent adjustments,
government policies (largely the NEP) were major destabilizers accentuating
and prolonging the province's economic difficulties. Conversely, Alberta's
resilience to the collapse of oil and agricultural prices in 1986 reflected a
combination of market and policy adjustments. The latter included large
reductions in energy taxes and royalties, significant agricultural assistance
programs, and reduction in the net flow of revenue to federal coffers.

The authors examine how to address instability in Alberta yet maintain a dynamic and competitive economy. No one policy response is viewed as sufficient, with industrial diversification seen as complementary to other initiatives. These include more attention to the regional macroeconomic impacts of federal tax and expenditure policies and, at the provincial level, through broadening and stabilizing the tax base of the Alberta economy, and by adopting a more countercyclical fiscal policy stance.

We believe that this study contributes importantly to a better understanding of Western Canadian economic issues.

Thomas E. Kierans
President and Chief Operating Officer
C.D. Howe Institute

Edward J. Chambers, Director
Western Centre for Economic Research
University of Alberta

October, 1990

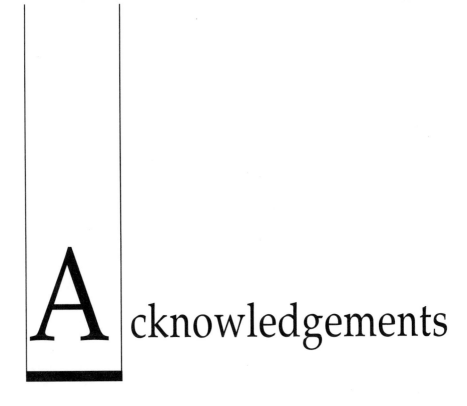

Acknowledgements

The authors would like to thank Ron Schlenker, Brian Lewis, and David Tims for their dedication and invaluable efforts as research assistants. We would also like to thank Jeanenne Hazard for assistance with the graphics work and Charlene Hill for manuscript preparation.

The Western Centre for Economic Reseach would like to thank the following agencies and groups for their financial support of this project: The Department of Regional Industrial Expansion, The Electrical Utility Planning Council of Alberta, and the Edmonton Economic Development Authority. Grants from the Winspear Foundation, Imperial Oil, NOVA Corporation, Potash Corporation of Saskatchewan, Banister Continental, Maclab Enterprises, Bumper Development Corporation, Chieftain International, Husky Oil, Alberta Energy contributed towards publication costs of this study.

1 Introduction

Key Issues

In 1982, after almost a decade of exceptionally strong performance, the Alberta economy suffered a reversal notable for its sharpness and persistence. Output fell by almost five percent (compared to a drop of slightly more than three percent nationally)[1] and did not show any significant recovery until 1985. Then, in 1986, adversity struck again. The collapse of oil and grain prices dealt a severe blow to the province's economic base and focused attention once again on the apparent instability and vulnerability of the Alberta economy and on the enormity of the associated social and economic costs.

Understandably, these events have led to renewed demands for policies to stabilize the economy. Based on the perception that the underlying problem is Alberta's narrow and highly variable petroleum and agriculture economic base, such demands typically focus on policies aimed at diversifying the economy. It is by no means clear, however, that this assessment of the problem, or the proposed solution, is accurate. Indeed, closer examination reveals many fundamental inconsistencies and, at the very least, gross oversimplification, in both the diagnosis and the proposed policy responses.

---

1. Based on data from Alberta Bureau of Statistics ASIST Matrix no. 6102, and Statistics Canada, CANSIM Matrix no. D20031.

Perhaps the most obvious inconsistency is the one between the actual and the predicted performance of the Alberta economy during the 1980s. For example, although the economic slump of 1986 can no doubt be attributed largely to the fall in grain and oil prices in conjunction with the province's specialization in energy and agriculture, this linkage cannot explain the extraordinary depth and length of the recession that began at the end of 1981. In fact, in the 1982-85 period, farm cash receipts remained fairly stable and the value of oil and gas production increased steadily, suggesting that, if anything, Alberta's economic downturn should have been considerably milder and shorter than that experienced in other regions. Similarly, the price/specialization linkage cannot explain the significant recovery experienced in the second half of 1987, when grain and natural-gas prices were still falling, and oil prices were at slightly more than half their 1985 level.[2] While such inconsistencies or enigmas do not necessarily mean that Alberta's narrow economic base is not a factor in the province's economic variability, they do raise some doubt as to whether it is the primary factor. At the very least, a complete accounting of the source of this instability is conspicuous by its absence, and, without such an accounting, it is impossible to devise effective stabilization policies.

Aside from the need for a more complete diagnosis of the problem, there are a number of rather fundamental questions and policy issues that must be addressed and that appear to have been largely ignored by the advocates of the diversification solution. Most notably, there is no clear definition of "diversification." It could mean expansion in the range of products produced by existing industries in the province; vertical integration and additional upgrading of primary products; diversification of the markets for the existing range of commodities produced in Alberta; or the introduction of new industries that exhibit either less variance than do the province's basic industries, or negative covariance with them (counter cyclical behavior), or both. Not surprisingly, in the absence of a clear definition confusion exists about both the diversification that is sought and the manner in which it can be achieved.

Another issue that is typically overlooked by proponents of diversification concerns the potential trade-off between per-capita income and greater stability. In general, specialization in the areas in which the province has a comparative advantage does promote higher incomes, but possibly at the expense of instability, which specialization can generate. And,

---

2. Data on farm cash receipts, value of oil and gas production, and oil and natural gas prices are from Statistics Canada, Cat. nos. 21-001 and 21-603 and Alberta Bureau of Statistics, ASIST Matrix nos. 6227 and 6228.

to the extent that diversification involves a shift into areas outside those that represent Alberta's comparative advantage, the cost of greater stability could well be a lower standard of living. In spite of its importance, this issue has not, to date, received much attention.

Finally, there are a variety of stabilization approaches other than diversification that tend to be ignored and that, at the very least, warrant investigation. If, as it is commonly believed, too great a reliance on resource sectors is at the root of Alberta's instability problem, then various sector-specific stabilization or insurance schemes may represent a viable and preferable alternative to diversification. There may also be room for improved macro stabilization policies at the regional level. For example, if Confederation is viewed as a mechanism that allows each region to specialize in its areas of comparative advantage and, via regional sharing, provides a buffer against the instability that such specialization may entail, part of the problem (and the solution) might be identified by means of a closer examination of the workings of that mechanism.

Objectives

The primary objectives of this study are to evaluate and diagnose Alberta's apparent problem of economic instability and to suggest some general directions for appropriate policy responses. We shall focus, specifically, on the following questions:

1. What factors account for the severity and length of the province's economic downturn in the early 1980s, on the one hand, and for the recent display of strength in adversity, on the other?

2. Is this variability an isolated event attributable to an unusual combination of factors that is unlikely to occur again, or is it simply the most recent manifestation of an inherent boom-bust cycle?

3. Given the identified sources of this instability, what are the appropriate policy responses?

Outline and Summary

Our analysis begins, in Chapter 2, with a diagnosis of the economic downturn. Proceeding from an overview of the performance and structure of the Alberta economy, we set out a general theoretical framework, and, within it, evaluate various existing explanations of the downturn. We conclude that, although many of the seeds for the economic bust were sown in the 1970s by predictable market forces and adjustments, government policy – especially the National Energy Program – played a role in accentuating and prolonging the province's economic difficulties.

In Chapter 3, we focus on the market and policy responses to the major economic adversities that the province has faced in the last few years, and on the contribution those responses may have made to the unexpected resilience of the economy. Using the theoretical framework developed in the preceding chapter, we examine the policy responses of the federal and provincial governments, along with the nature and effects of a variety of market adjustments, market-induced structural changes, and provincial initiatives to diversify the economy. Although many of the responses and effects will become apparent only as additional data for the post-1986 period become available, the results of our analysis suggest that three particularly important factors have contributed to Alberta's remarkable performance in face of significant adversity. The first is a combination of policy and market adjustments specific to the province's key resource sectors, including large reductions in energy taxes and royalties, very significant agricultural assistance programs (combined with strong markets for livestock and livestock products), and substantial reductions in production costs, especially in the energy sector. The second is the nature of changes in the overall fiscal-policy stance, as measured by the difference between federal government revenues collected in Alberta and federal expenditures, in or transfers to, the provincial economy. Although the overall level of these balances, especially with regard to federal policies, has worked to retard rather than to stimulate the Alberta economy, there are indications that the direction of change has been a positive factor. Finally, there is evidence that, as a result of market adjustments, provincial policies, and a variety of factors that have encouraged high levels of entrepreneurship, significant progress has been made in market and intra-industry diversification, and in the development of new industries.

In Chapter 4, we examine the issue of instability in the Alberta economy within a longer time frame, addressing two questions in particular:

1.   Going beyond this latest boom-bust cycle, how does the Alberta economy measure-up to other regions in the degree of its inherent instability? and

2.   What are the primary sources of this variability?

After distinguishing among the various types of instability and establishing the relevant measures, we present the results of a statistical analysis. In general, we conclude that, in terms of most measures and relative to the other provincial economies, the degree of economic instability in Alberta ranks at or near the top and that a significant portion of this high variability can be attributed to the unusually large swings experienced over the last decade. Moreover, the economy of Alberta exhibits significantly more instability than that of either Oklahoma or Texas, two U.S. states that share many of Alberta's structural characteristics. To identify the sources of this variability in the Alberta economy, we undertake a sectoral disaggregation of the index of economic instability, which reveals that, relative to the situation in the more stable regional economies, Alberta's construction sector (and the corresponding investment component of GDP) is particularly unstable; the variability in employment is very high in all sectors, including the government sector; there is an unusually small number of cases in which the sectors tend to vary in opposite directions; and, contrary to the common view, fluctuations in Alberta's exports are not the main source of the instability. In summary, it appears that the province's problem of economic variability is indeed serious and goes well beyond the most recent economic downturn.

The issue of what can be done to reduce this provincial instability is taken up in Chapter 5. After assessing the demand for policies to deal with the problem, we present and discuss the main approaches that might potentially address it, including the Confederation approach (greater attention to interregional transfers and the effects of the regional distribution of federal fiscal balances); provincial government stabilization by means of enhanced countercyclical fiscal policy and sector-specific stabilization schemes; industrial diversification; and policies aimed at encouraging individuals and firms in the province to adopt behavior more consistent with high levels of uncertainty and economic instability (for example, encouraging high saving rates and low debt-equity ratios).

According to a survey of attitudes toward the issue of economic instability, Albertans apparently feel strongly that something needs to be done and that the solution should involve diversifying the economy. However, as indicated by the analysis presented in the preceding chapters and by our general discussion of the various approaches to achieving greater stability, it is far from clear that diversification can be considered a panacea. Rather, it should be viewed primarily as a complement to strategies on other fronts. For example, there is considerable scope for increasing stability simply through greater attention to the regional macroeconomic impacts of federal tax-and-expenditure policies. Similarly, substantial improvements can be achieved by broadening and stabilizing the Alberta government's tax base and by adopting a much more countercyclical fiscal-policy stance. In addition, much could be gained by avoiding policies that have the effect of **engendering**, rather than discouraging, the kind of behavior among individuals and firms that is based too heavily on extrapolative expectations and too little on the maxim of "preparing for the worst and hoping for the best."

With regard to diversification, we conclude that it is unrealistic to focus strictly on the development of new industries characterized by low variance or negative covariance with those that form the province's economic base. Instead, the adoption of a very broad definition of diversification – one that includes diversification of markets and expanded product lines for existing industries, vertical integration, and resource upgrading, along with "industrial diversification" – in which the objective is to broaden and expand, rather than to change, the province's economic base, seems much preferable. Further, in pursuing this objective, it would appear that policies aimed at creating a favorable environment, addressing market imperfections, and "creating" comparative advantage (for example, through research-and-development initiatives) are generally more effective than those aimed at "picking winners."

2 Diagnosing Alberta's Downturn

The social and economic costs associated with the vulnerability and instability of the Alberta economy since the early 1980s are considerably more apparent than are either the fundamental causes or the appropriate policy responses. Indeed, at least in terms of the theories typically used to diagnose the problem and recommend solutions, many aspects of the behavior of the province's economy over this period are puzzling.[1] On the one hand, there is the view, perhaps best expressed by the Economic Council of Canada,[2] that the Alberta economy has become increasingly diversified and less dependent on the fortunes of the resource sector and that it is inherently only slightly more variable than that of Ontario, the benchmark province. Although this might account for the surprising resiliency of the province's economy in the face of the dramatic collapse of oil and grain prices in 1986, it cannot explain the sharp downturn and prolonged weakness that preceded that event.

1. This puzzling behavior is also evidenced by the frequency of extremely large errors in forecasts. For example, in March 1986, it was forecast that, on the basis of oil at $18 (U.S.) per barrel, Alberta's real GDP would increase by 4.2 percent in 1986 and 1.2 percent in 1987. Then, in January 1987, a 2.9 percent drop in real GDP was forecast for 1987. See the Conference Board of Canada, *Provincial Outlook*, March 1986, p. 30, and Winter 1986-87, p. 17. Current estimates reveal that Alberta's real GDP declined by 1.1 percent in 1986 and increased by about 0.5 percent in 1987.

2. Economic Council of Canada, *Western Transition* (Ottawa: Supply and Services, 1984), pp. 13, 197.

At the other extreme is the view that Alberta's economy is still almost exclusively driven by its agriculture and energy industries and, hence, that its performance remains tightly bound to the vagaries of internationally determined resource prices. Although this model can explain the reversal in 1986, it cannot explain why that reversal was not more devastating or why the downturn that began in the early 1980s was as deep and lengthy as it was.

Clearly, before an effective policy response can be devised, it is necessary to reconcile such discrepancies or, more precisely, to develop a more consistent and complete explanation of the observed behavior of the Alberta economy. The development of such an explanation is the main objective in this chapter. We shall first present an overview of the performance and structure of the provincial economy and outline the theory that explains the behavior of small, open regional economies, then proceed to a general diagnosis of Alberta's downturn.

Performance and Structure of the Alberta Economy: An Overview

Before an accurate diagnosis can be made, it is necessary to establish the facts with regard to Alberta's economic performance and structure. We shall first evaluate the province's recent economic performance relative to that of earlier periods and that of the nation, then outline various structural aspects of its economy that might promote an understanding of key driving forces and linkages and provide clues to the fundamental causes of the economic downturn.

General Performance

One of the broadest measures of economic activity is real Gross Domestic Product (GDP). As illustrated in Figure 1, Alberta's economic performance since the early 1980s in terms of GDP, stands in sharp contrast to that of previous periods. In particular, the persistent weakness since 1982 represents a significant divergence from the above-average performance of the previous two decades. Even before energy prices soared in the 1970s, the Alberta economy generally outperformed its national counterpart, in spite of declining oil and gas prices (in real terms) over most of the 1960s.[3]

Ultimately, however, the economic performance of a region is not judged by the value of production within its geographical boundaries (that is, GDP),

---

3. The average price of western crude oil (measured in 1947 dollars per m3 at the wellhead) was $11.67 in 1951, $10.71 in 1956, $9.41 in 1961, $9.10 in 1966, and $8.49 in 1971 (Canadian Petroleum Association, *Statistical Handbook, 1988*).

Figure 1. Real GDP Growth Rates, Canada and Alberta, 1961–1987

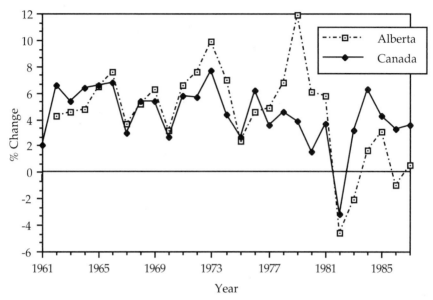

Source: Statistics Canada (61-510 and Cansim D20031) and Alberta Bureau of Statistics (Alberta Economic Accounts, various years and October 1987 update)

but by the degree of economic welfare that this production affords its residents.[4] Three broad indicators of Alberta's performance from this vantage point are presented in Figures 2 to 5. As shown, the province's relative per-capita income position improved significantly after the late 1970s (from its long-term position of rough equality with the national average)[5] and then declined sharply after 1982. However, as indicated by the much larger and more pronounced shifts in employment and unemployment, as well as in net migration, these variations in per-capita income disguise many elements that are more closely associated with regional adjustment and economic welfare. In this regard, it might be pointed out that, by 1985, well before the collapse of grain and oil prices, employment in Alberta was still about 2.5 percent below its 1981 level, while, in the nation, it was 2.8 percent

4. In the case of Alberta, there is a very large gap between GDP and income received. For example, in 1985 personal income in Alberta was 65 percent of the province's GDP, whereas for Canada the comparable figure was 85 percent. This large difference is related to the very high level of capital intensity of production in Alberta (especially in agriculture and mining), the high levels of ownership outside Alberta, and the fact that, unlike other provinces, Alberta is a very efficient collector of economic rents.

5. See Robert L. Mansell, "Canadian Regional Inequity: The Process of Adjustment" (Ph.D. diss., University of Alberta, 1975).

Figure 2. Alberta Per Capita Personal Income Relative to National Average

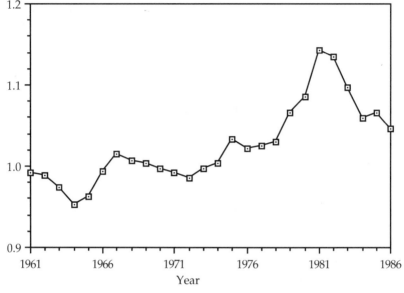

Source: Statistics Canada (13-201).

Figure 3. Percentage Change in Employment, Canada and Alberta, 1961-1987

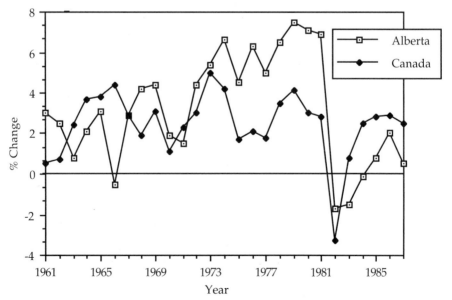

Source: Statistics Canada (71-201).

Figure 4. Unemployment Rate, Canada and Alberta, 1961-1987

Source: Statistics Canada (71-201).

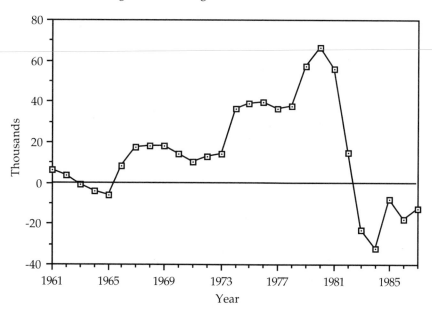

Figure 5. Net Migration To (From) Alberta

Source: Alberta Bureau of Statistics (ASIST 6128 and 6354).

above the 1981 pre-recession high. Also, for the first time in many decades, Alberta's unemployment rate had risen above the national average – despite a net outflow of more than 63,000 people from the province between 1983 and 1985. These statistics portray a much sharper and, in terms of social costs, much more serious reversal than the drop in relative per-capita income might imply.

One of the more sensitive indicators of the overall economic condition of a region is change in housing prices. Because housing is not a commodity that can be traded across regional boundaries, many of the spillover effects that normally accompany interregional trade are absent, and prices are therefore largely a function of economic conditions and expectations specific to the region.[6] In addition, since the bulk of the average family's net worth is located in home equity, variations in housing prices are also indicative of changes in wealth. These, in turn, have many important implications, – in the case of Alberta, most obviously for regionally-based financial institutions, many of which have failed.[7] Significant and prolonged declines in housing prices can quickly generate negative housing equity which, in combination with substantial declines in employment and generally declining real-asset prices, can dramatically reduce the value of a regional financial institution's asset base.

As is evident from Figure 6, the behavior of housing prices in Alberta corresponds generally to patterns indicated by the other indices that we have just previously outlined. What is perhaps most interesting, however, is that the increases during the pre-1981 period are not out of line with those that occurred in other provinces. This seems to conflict with the commonly held view that, in Alberta, these increases were associated primarily with the capitalization of energy rents in housing prices. What **is** out of line, on the other hand, is the number of residential mortgage foreclosures that have occurred. As shown in Figure 7, more than 45,000 statements of claim and more than 28,000 final foreclosure orders were issued in Alberta between 1982 and the end of 1987. In any case, it is readily apparent from both the behavior of housing prices and the number of mortgage foreclosures that,

---

6. It should, however, be noted that the prices of the material components of housing are subject to such interregional spillovers.

7. They include the following: Dial Mortgage Corporation Ltd.; Battleford Mortgage; Ram Mortgage Corporation Ltd.; Tower Mortgage Ltd.; Fidelity Trust; Heritage Savings and Trust Company and North West Trust Company; the Canadian Commercial Bank; the Northlands Bank; and First Investors Corporation Ltd. and Associated Investors of Canada Ltd. In addition, since 1984, the Alberta government has placed almost a third of the province's credit unions under supervision, forced a number of credit union amalgamations, and provided substantial deposit guarantees and injections for credit unions. While some of these failures or near collapses can no doubt be blamed on poor management, there is obviously a fundamental problem that goes beyond the issue of management skills.

Figure 6. Historical Canadian Housing Prices

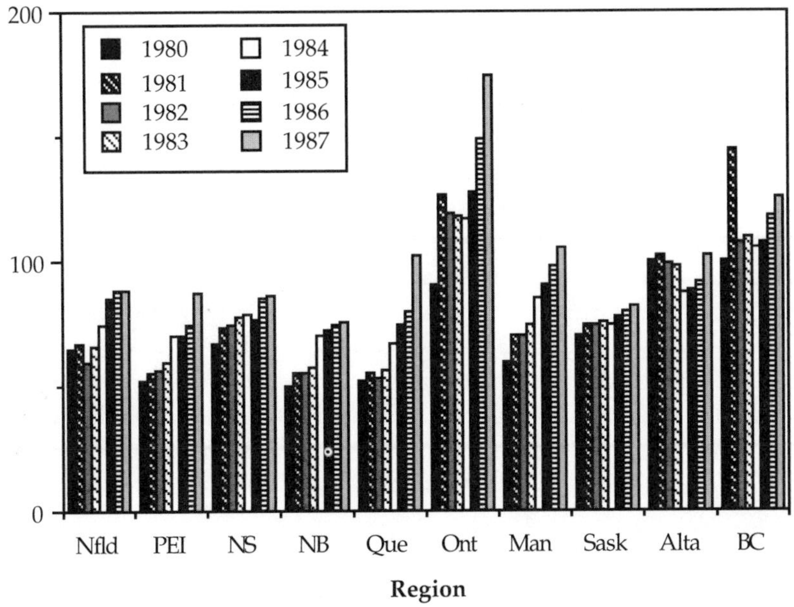

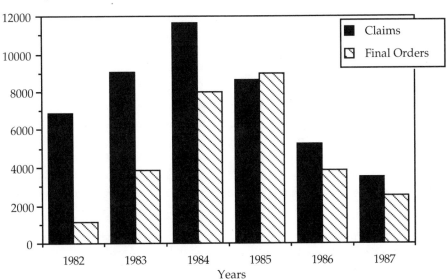

200
100
0
1980
1981
1982
1983
1984
1985
1986
1987
Nfld
PEI
NS
NB
Que
Ont
Man
Sask
Alta
BC
Region

Source: Royal LePage Survey of Canadian House Prices, various issues. Prices shown are averages for a standard detached bungalow (see survey for specifications) in major regional cities.

Figure 7. Residential Mortgage Foreclosures in Alberta, 1982-1987

12000
10000
8000
6000
4000
2000
0
Claims
Final Orders
1982
1983
1984
1985
1986
1987
Years

Source: Alberta Municipal Affairs, Housing Division.

relative to the other provinces, Alberta's economic performance has been weak, and the resulting costs, very high.

A few general observations on Alberta's economic performance in recent years might be useful here. First, the post-1981 period unquestionably represents a sharp departure from the three preceding decades, when the province's performance was generally equal to or better than the national average. Although there were significant downturns during the 1950-80 period, they tended to be consistent with national fluctuations and, unlike the situation in the 1980s, there were no lengthy periods during which the province's economic performance was substantially below the nation's. A comparison of Alberta's earlier oil and gas boom (late 1940s to mid-1950s) with the more recent one (1973-81) is also revealing: in both cases, the provincial economy demonstrated strong, above-average performance, but the similarity ends there. There was no dramatic and prolonged downturn relative to national performance after the earlier boom, as there was in the post-1981 period, even though a national recession occurred at the end of each one.

All of this suggests that the serious economic reversal that began in 1982 is attributable to factors that go beyond those associated with explanations focusing on resource-sector booms and busts. This observation is also supported by comparisons of Alberta's economic performance in recent years with that of three U.S. states – Oklahoma, Texas, and Colorado – which have roughly comparable petroleum and agriculture economic bases.[8] As shown in Figure 8, Alberta's post-1981 economic reversal was, as measured by increases in the unemployment rate, considerably sharper and more prolonged than that experienced by its U.S. counterparts. It is also interesting to note that in 1986, with the collapse of energy prices, Alberta's unemployment rate declined, albeit slightly, while in all three U.S. states it rose significantly (even though, nationally, the U.S. unemployment rate continued to fall).

Furthermore, especially since mid 1987, the provincial economy has shown surprising strength, particularly in light of the fact that grain and natural-gas prices continued to fall over most of the year, and oil prices had recovered to just over half their 1985 level. For example, 1987 employment was up slightly over 1986 levels, and the unemployment rate continued to fall. Whether this reflects the fundamental strength of the economy or simply

---

8. As indicated by the values of sectoral location quotients, Alberta and these three U.S. states all exhibit specialization in agriculture, mining (mainly oil and gas), and related processing activities. The main difference is that, relative to its U.S. counterparts, Alberta has proportionately less manufacturing. For a detailed comparison of the Alberta and Texas economies, see Robert L. Mansell, "Texas and Alberta: A Comparison of Regional Economies," *Texas Business Review* 55 (1981): 241-246.

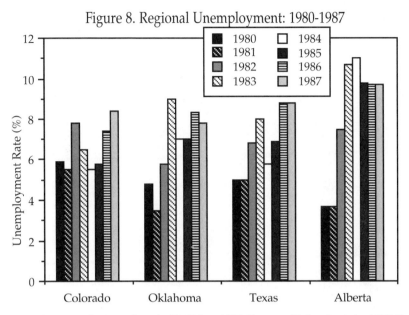

Figure 8. Regional Unemployment: 1980-1987

Source: Statistics Canada (71-201) and U.S. Bureau of Labor Statistics (6742.2).

the results of various lags and short-run policy shifts is a matter that we shall take up in a later section.

Structural Aspects

Underlying the macroeconomic performance described above are a variety of structural elements and shifts that can provide important clues to the causes of Alberta's downturn. For example, as illustrated in Figure 9, one of the most notable shifts has been in the relative size of the investment (or real-capital formation) component of real GDP. The steady increase from about 23 percent of GDP in the late 1960s and early 1970s to 38 percent in 1981, then back to about 21 percent by 1986, suggests that both the rapid economic expansion of the 1970s and the subsequent downturn in 1982 were very much an investment-related phenomenon.

It is also interesting to note that imports have tended to rise significantly during periods of strong economic growth in the province and fall during periods of decline or slow growth. This kind of behavior is predicted by economic theory and reveals that imports are an important automatic stabilizer for the Alberta economy.[9] It can also be observed that, except in

9. In a downturn the leakage of regional income associated with imports is decreased and, consequently, the decline in economic activity is less than it would otherwise be. In an upturn caused, for example, by a rise in investment the effect is to dampen the increase in economic activity.

Figure 9. Final Demand Components of Alberta Real GDP

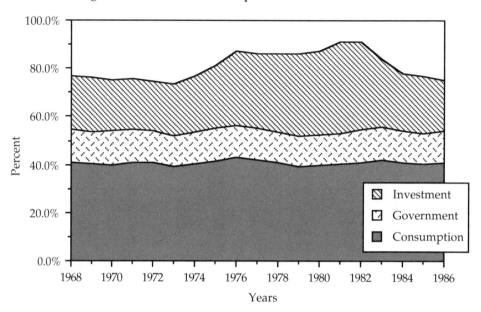

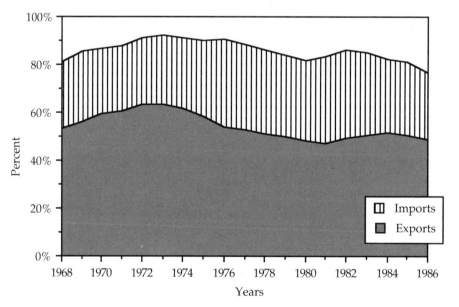

Source: Alberta Bureau of Statistics, Alberta Economic Accounts.

Figure 10. Value of Alberta Exports and Imports, 1968-1986

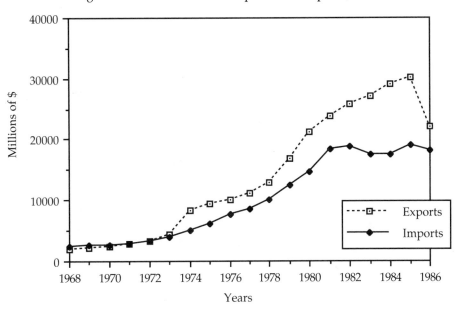

Source: Alberta Bureau of Statistics, Alberta Economic Accounts.

1986, the contribution of exports to GDP (measured in real or constant dollars) has remained fairly stable; hence variations in the volume of exports have not been a primary factor in the wide swings in Alberta's economic performance. Nevertheless, as shown in Figure 10, there is an important price dimension that is typically overlooked in regional analysis. That is, with the substantial increase in Alberta's net terms of trade (the ratio of export to import price indices), the province has, since 1975, run a sizable trade surplus. The implications of this are discussed in a later section. Here it will suffice to note that, unless there are offsetting financial capital outflows or interregional fiscal transfers, such a surplus must result in a positive shift in economic activity and real wealth to the province.

Another view of Alberta's economic structure (and of changes within it) is presented in Figures 11 and 12. It leads to the following observations. First, although the mining sector (which consists mostly of the oil and gas industries) directly accounts for less than six percent of total employment, its overall importance to the economy is substantially larger. It directly accounts for more than a third of Alberta's GDP and, when the indirect or linkage effects are taken into account, its contribution to both GDP and employment is even greater. For example, in 1981, about half of the construction activity and one-quarter of the manufacturing activity in the province were related to

Figure 11. Sectoral Shares of Alberta GDP, 1968-1986

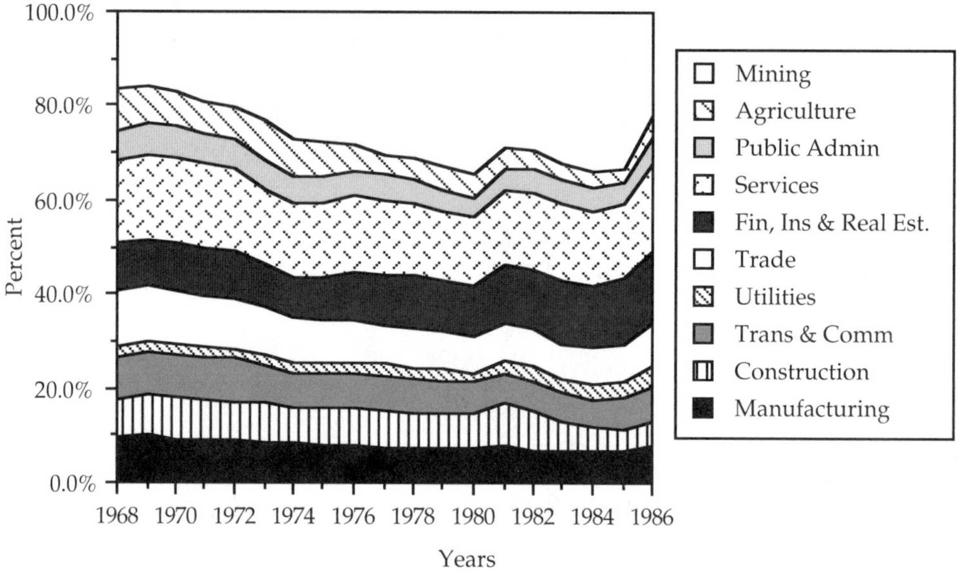

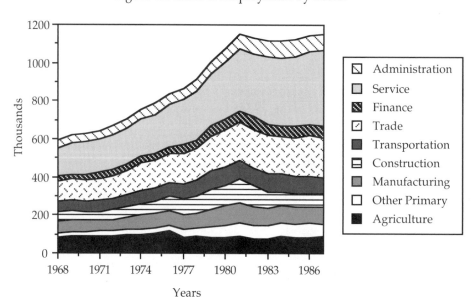

Source: Alberta Bureau of Statistics, Alberta Economic Accounts.

Figure 12. Alberta Employment by Sector

Source: Alberta Bureau of Statistics, Alberta Economic Accounts.

oil and gas.[10] Thus, about 70 percent of Alberta's commodity production can be tied to the energy sector. And, when its purchases of services and its large contributions to provincial government revenues are included,[11] the conclusion that the energy sector is the major driving force in the Alberta economy becomes inescapable.

Similarly, the relatively small employment and GDP shares for agriculture greatly understate the importance of that sector. Indeed, an analysis of input-output coefficients and sectoral multipliers reveals that agriculture, along with energy, dominates the list of industries in Alberta that have the strongest forward and backward linkages.[12] As illustrated in Table 1, the agriculture and energy sectors also occupy a key position in the composition of Alberta's commodity exports.

With regard to shifts in the structure of the provincial economy during the 1970s and early 1980s, it is evident that, in terms of output in value added, Alberta has become increasingly dependent on the oil and gas sector, and in terms of employment, on the services sector (see Table 2). Moreover, it would appear at first glance that the rapid growth of the energy and construction sectors during the 1970s may have caused some displacement of other activities, producing a more specialized and less diversified provincial economy. For example, as shown in Table 2, with the exception of finance, insurance, and real estate, the relative contribution to GDP of all sectors declined. This could, however, be a statistical illusion, in the sense that a large increase in the share of the mining sector (related mostly to changes in the energy-rents component of value added) must entail smaller shares for other sectors, even though, in absolute terms, they had grown rapidly. Moreover, similar shifts may have been taking place at the national level, in which case no such conclusion would be justified.

---

10. See Alberta, *Science and Technology Development in Alberta: A Discussion Paper* (Edmonton: Government of Alberta, March 1984), Appendix 1, p. 34.

11. In 1985, oil, gas, and gas byproduct royalties (net of incentives and credits), along with land bonuses and rentals, amounted to 47 percent of the Alberta government's total revenues. See Alberta, Alberta Treasury, *Financial Summary and Budgeting Review, 1985-1986* (Edmonton: Alberta Treasury, n.d.), p. 34.

12. Alberta's six most heavily backward-linked industries (that is, the industries that made the largest purchases from other industries in the province) are food and beverages; petroleum and coal products; chemical and chemical products; agriculture; forestry; and mineral fuels. The province's most heavily forward-linked industries (that is, the industries that make the largest sales to other Alberta industries) are food and beverages; mineral fuels; agriculture; construction; chemical and chemical products; and petroleum and coal products. See Mansell, "Texas and Alberta," p. 243.

Table 1. Composition of Alberta's Commodity Exports, 1985 and 1986
($ millions and percent of total exports)

Commodity	1985		1986	
Live animals	$106.1	0.8%	$115.7	1.1%
Grains	1,291.4	9.4	1,047.3	10.0
Meat	143.3	1.0	175.4	1.7
Other agricultural products	53.8	0.4	53.6	0.5
Coal	360.9	2.6	326.3	3.1
Crude petroleum	4,401.4	32.2	2,874.9	27.4
Natural gas and sulfur	4,220.0	30.9	3,169.5	30.2
Chemicals, fertilizers, petroleum, and coal products	1,711.7	12.5	1,325.2	12.6
Other	1,385.5	10.1	1,396.4	13.3
Total	**13,674.1**		**10,484.3**	

Source: Based on data from Alberta Bureau of Statistics, ASIST Matrix no.6280.

Table 2. Sectoral Shares of Alberta's Gross Domestic Product and Employment, 1971, 1981, and 1986
(percentage)

Sector	Gross Domestic Product			Employment		
	1971	1981	1986	1971	1981	1986
Agriculture and forestry	6.4%	4.3%	4.6%	14.6%	7.6%	7.6%
Mining	16.9	28.9	21.9	3.7	6.1	6.1
Manufacturing	9.0	8.0	7.8	8.9	9.2	7.8
Construction	8.4	8.9	5.1	6.8	10.6	5.8
Transportation, communications, and utilities	11.5	9.0	11.7	8.9	8.4	8.1
Trade	10.7	8.1	9.0	18.2	17.6	18.7
Finance, insurance, and real estate	10.0	12.6	15.6	5.1	5.2	5.1
Community, business, and personal services	18.5	15.5	18.3	27.2	28.0	33.4
Public administration	6.6	4.7	5.9	6.4	7.3	7.4

Source: Based on data from Alberta Buru of Statistics, ASIST Matrix no. 6101; and Statistics Canada, *The Labour Force*, Cat. no. 71-001, various issues.

Table 3. Location Quotients: Various Sectors' Shares of the Alberta Economy, 1973-1987

(as a ratio of the Canadian average; Canada = 1.00)

	Agri-culture	Mining	Con-struction	Manu-facturing	Transport. & Utilities	Trade	Finance	Services	Govern-ment
1973	2.45	2.63	1.18	0.41	1.00	1.09	1.06	1.03	0.96
1974	2.40	2.68	1.22	0.42	1.02	1.13	0.95	1.00	0.99
1975	2.59	2.37	1.25	0.43	1.00	1.06	0.89	0.96	1.01
1976	2.67	2.50	1.37	0.43	0.96	1.04	0.87	0.97	0.97
1977	1.99	2.94	1.47	0.44	1.00	1.09	0.97	0.97	0.93
1978	1.82	3.53	1.60	0.41	1.06	1.03	0.94	0.99	0.92
1979	1.71	3.60	1.78	0.41	1.06	1.04	.101	0.97	0.90
1980	1.65	3.24	1.65	0.47	1.06	1.05	0.96	0.96	0.93
1981	1.62	3.28	1.79	0.47	1.01	1.03	0.97	0.94	1.00
1982	1.46	3.60	1.76	0.46	1.01	1.02	1.065	0.95	1.03
1983	1.51	3.74	1.50	0.43	1.05	1.05	0.98	0.99	1.04
1984	1.71	3.91	1.23	0.44	1.09	1.00	0.91	1.02	1.06
1985	1.62	3.69	1.17	0.44	1.05	1.03	0.96	1.01	1.11
1986	1.69	3.73	1.08	0.43	1.05	1.04	0.90	1.03	1.08
1987	1.81	3.66	1.10	0.43	1.01	1.02	0.87	1.05	1.07

Sources: Calculated using data from Statistics Canada, *The Labour Force,* Cat. no. 71-001, various issues; and idem, *Labour Force Annual Averages, 1975-1983,* Cat. no. 71-529 (Ottawa, 1984).

To take these factors into account, sectoral-employment location quotients[13] (percentages of regional employment in a given sector relative to percentages of national employment in the same sector) were computed, and are shown in Table 3. As indicated by the location quotients that exceed one, the provincial economy relative to the national exhibits a strong specialization in agriculture, mining, and construction, and a somewhat lesser one in trade and transportation, communications and utilities. Furthermore, although the Alberta economy became increasingly specialized in mining and construction during the 1970s and early 1980s, it is not clear that there was an accompanying reduction in the relative positions of other sectors (such as manufacturing) that typically signify a diversified economy. In fact, it would appear that, if anything, the opposite occurred. That is, the increased specialization in oil and gas brought gains to other sectors, such as construction, manufacturing, and services. The Economic Council of Canada,

---

13. Location quotients based on employment rather than GDP are used to avoid the problems associated with the large swings in the energy-rents component of GDP over this period.

making the same observation, concluded that "the Alberta economy diversified a great deal throughout the 1970s."[14] To the extent that the growth in these other sectors was directly tied to the growth in input requirements of the mining and construction sectors, however, this does not represent the kind of diversification that lessens the provincial economy's sensitivity to swings in the primary sectors.

Analytical Framework

In developing a logical and internally consistent explanation of Alberta's economic performance and its underlying structural elements, it is necessary to work within the framework of economic theory to establish key linkages and directions of causality. In this section, we shall present the main elements of economic theory that are relevant to the operation of a small, open, regional economy, with a view to isolating the causal factors that warrant special attention *vis-a-vis* Alberta's economic downturn and the province's resilience in face of the collapse of energy and grain prices in 1986.

Staple Theory and Export-Base Models

Two models commonly used to explain economic upturns and downturns in Canada's peripheral regions are the staple theory[15] and the economic- or export-base models.[16] Although there are some differences in the specific mechanisms involved, both theories focus on the role of exports, especially of primary products, as the main determinant of regional growth or decline. For example, according to the staple theory, a rise in the price of a region's resource product creates an incentive for its exploitation and export. Capital and labor are thus attracted to the region, and further expansion occurs through the development of backward linkages to supply and transportation industries, forward linkages to processing industries, and final-demand linkages involving the supply of goods and services to the local population.

14. Economic Council of Canada, *Western Transition*, p. 152.

15. Associated with Harold Innis, *The Fur Trade in Canada: An Introduction To Canadian Economic History* (Toronto: Oxford University Press, 1927) and *The Cod Fisheries: The History of an International Economy* (New Haven, CT: Carnegie Endowment for International Peace, Division of Economics and History, 1940); see W. A. MacKintosh, "Some Aspects of a Pioneer Economy," *Canadian Journal of Economics and Political Science* 2 (1936): 457-463, and M. H. Watkins, "A Staple Theory of Economic Growth," *Canadian Journal of Economics and Political Science* 29 (1963): 141-158.

16. Douglas C. North, "Location Theory and Regional Economic Growth," *Journal of Political Economy* 62 (1955): 243-258; see also J. C. Stabler, "Export and Evolution: The Process of Regional Change," *Land Economics* 44 (1968): 11-23.

According to these theories, then, the primary causes of shifts in a region's economic fortunes are to be found in changes in the prices of, and the demands for, its basic resources.

An extension from this general approach, developed by Robert Mansell, focuses on a region's resource base as the main determinant of its overall economic performance.[17] For example, Mansell suggests that the remarkable long-run similarities in growth rates and levels of per-capita income prior to 1981 in Alberta and Texas (relative to their national counterparts), in spite of quite different historical, political, and economic environments, may in large part be due to resource-base similarities. The closeness of the two economies in character – independent, risk-taking, and highly mobile labor forces – and industrial structures – both are characterized by industries closely linked to petroleum and agriculture – may be due mostly to the simple fact that both developed around similar agricultural and petroleum resource bases. This, in combination with external influences (e.g., national policies and internationally determined commodity prices), would in turn explain similarities in economic performance.

There are obvious weaknesses in these theories, particularly in the context of shorter-run variations in regional economic activity. Nevertheless, they draw attention to the potential role of resource prices and policies and changes in the level of exports in explaining Alberta's economic reversal.

Keynesian Models

Within a Keynesian framework, the economic fortunes of a region are determined mainly by changes in aggregate demand. The latter is defined as: c (consumption) + i (investment) + g (government expenditures on goods and services) + x (exports) – m (imports). The levels of c and m are primarily determined (endogenously) by the levels of income and economic activity in the region, and i is a function of interest rates, expected returns, changes in infrastructure requirements and capacity utilization, and so on. In the Keynesian framework, as in the staple theory and export-base models, exports represent an important driving force and are heavily influenced by both the level of economic activity in other regions and the behavior of the region's export prices. Changes in both investment and government expenditure, however, also represent important driving forces in this framework. Furthermore, in all cases, there are multiplier and

---

17. Mansell, "Texas and Alberta"; idem, "Energy Policy, Prices and Rents: Implications for Regional Growth and Development," in *Still Living Together: Present Trends and Future Directions in Canadian Regional Development*, ed. W. J. Coffey and M. Polese (Montreal: Institute for Research on Public Policy, 1987).

multiplier-accelerator mechanisms[18] that amplify the effects of shifts in the main exogenous components of aggregate demand (that is, in i, g, and x).

Three dimensions of the Keynesian framework are particularly important in a regional context. First, the (positive or negative) multiplier effects associated with a change in, say, investment or exports really have three components. As incomes in the region grow, so do consumption and, in many cases, investment and government spending, leading to the Keynesian multiplier effect. In addition, there is the so-called Leontief component that operates through interindustry purchases. For example, as one industry expands, there is an increased demand for inputs from other industries in the region, and this in turn leads to successive rounds of expansion for those related industries. Finally, there is a population component that operates through interregional migration. With a general increase in aggregate demand, unemployment in the region falls while, relative to the situation in other regions, per-capita income and wage levels rise. This leads to net in-migration, which, in turn, creates new demands for consumer items, housing, and public infrastructure. It will suffice to note at this point that, taken together, these multiplier effects can be large, especially in an economy like Alberta's, where migration flows are very sensitive to changes in relative economic performance. Furthermore, these multipliers operate in both directions.

The second relevant aspect of the Keynesian framework is that it demonstrates that both federal and provincial fiscal policies play an important role in determining the level of economic activity in a region. If, for example, the provincial government runs a fiscal deficit (that is, collects less in revenue than it spends on goods and services or transfer payments), the effect, at least in the short run, is to stimulate the regional economy. Although typically overlooked, the federal fiscal position with regard to a region is even more important.[19] For example, if the federal government runs a fiscal surplus (that is, collects more in revenues in a region than it returns via spending in and transfers to that region), the effect is to deflate the economy.

The third important dimension involves regional balance-of-payments adjustments. Although this issue has received some well-deserved attention

18. The accelerator effect operates through the relationship between changes in the level of output on income and the level of investment. Thus, if the rate of growth in output falls, even though it still shows positive growth, the level of investment will decline and this will produce a multiplied, negative effect on the economy.

19. For example, the stimulative effects of a provincial-government deficit will be partly offset by the increased taxes or reduced levels of provincial-government services that must ensue to cover the higher interest and principal repayment expenditures associated with the increased debt. When the federal government runs a fiscal deficit with a region, however, these offsetting factors are much smaller, because a significant part of the higher debt costs are borne by residents of other regions.

in recent years,[20] it too has generally been overlooked in regional applications of Keynesian theory. Regional balance-of-payments adjustments are not easily observed (since balance-of-payments accounting is not typically applied to interregional transfers of commodities and funds), but they are even more direct than are national adjustments. Since a common currency is involved, there can be no exchange-rate adjustments to regional balance-of-payments surpluses and deficits. Thus, in the absence of offsetting federal fiscal balances, a surplus must lead directly to a transfer of real wealth and activity to the region (via changes in the ownership of financial claims and changes in wage, price, employment, and income levels),[21] while a deficit must produce the opposite effect. In any case, it is evident that, in diagnosing Alberta's economic reversal, attention must be paid to shifts in the province's trade and payments balances, as well as to the regional distribution of federal fiscal balances.

General Equilibrium Models

In recent years, a variety of general-equilibrium models have been developed and used to explain regional economic behavior in Canada.[22] In general, these models incorporate many of the adjustments already discussed (that is, adjustments involving shifts in aggregate demand, and interregional movements of people, commodities, and funds) but differ in a number of important respects. In particular, they tend to have a Neoclassical thrust (that is, they hold that the behavior of economic agents is based on profit and

---

20. See A. P. Thirlwall, "Regional Problems Are Balance of Payments Problems," *Regional Studies* 14 (1980): 419-425; Thomas J. Courchene, "Avenues of Adjustment: The Transfer System and Regional Disparities," in *Canadian Confederation at the Crossroads*, ed. M. Walker (Vancouver: Fraser Institute, 1978); idem., "The National Energy Program and Fiscal Federation: Some Observations," in *Reaction: The National Energy Program*, ed. G. C. Watkins and M. A. Walker (Vancouver: Fraser Institute, 1981); idem., "A Market Perspective on Regional Disparities," *Canadian Public Policy* 7 (1981): 506-518.

21. The extent to which this transfer is effected via changes in wage and price levels versus changes in real variables, such as employment, will depend on the relative flexibility of these variables. Since wages and prices tend to be upwardly flexible but downwardly rigid, a regional balance-of-payments surplus usually leads to adjustments in the form of increases in price variables more than in employment, while a deficit leads to adjustments in the form of decreases in employment more than in price variables.

22. See, for example, K. H. Norrie and M. B. Percy, *Energy Price Increases, Economic Rents and Industrial Structure in a Small Regional Economy*, Discussion Paper no. 201 (Ottawa: Economic Council of Canada, 1982); idem., *Economic Rents, Province-Building and Interregional Adjustment: A Two-Region General Equilibrium Analysis*, Discussion Paper no. 230 (Ottawa: Economic Council of Canada, 1983); John Whalley and Irene Trela, *Regional Aspects of Confederation*, Royal Commission on the Economic Union and Development Prospects for Canada, vol. 68 (Toronto: University of Toronto Press, 1986); and F. J. Anderson, *Regional Economic Analysis: A Canadian Perspective* (Toronto: Harcourt Brace Jovanovich, Canada, 1988).

utility maximization), they pay more attention to the supply side and the need for relationships to balance when aggregated across all regions, and they allow for intersectoral shifts. The greatest appeal of these models, however, is that they are able to address many of the issues highlighted by the staple theory and the Keynesian models.

With the exception of a recent work by John Whalley and Irene Trela and several similar efforts focusing on issues related to trade,[23] most of these models have not been "applied" in the sense of being fitted to historical data. Nevertheless, they do provide important insights, particularly with regard to structural changes. For example, the results obtained by K. H. Norrie and M. B. Percy suggest that an energy-based regional economy will experience "Dutch disease" – increased specialization or reduced diversification – following an increase in energy prices, and a reversal of Dutch disease, or market-induced diversification, after a fall in energy prices.[24] In general, this occurs because, in the case of an energy-price increase, wages and input prices are bid up by the expansion of the energy sector and related sectors. This puts downward pressure on output and employment in those sectors, which, because of import competition, cannot pass these higher costs along in the form of higher prices. Hence, an increase in resource prices generally causes the region to become more specialized in primary production, while a decrease produces the opposite effect.

The general-equilibrium modelling framework is very useful in understanding a number of distinctive features of resource-based economies such as Alberta's. For example, Alberta has tended to become more specialized during booms in resource sectors and less so during slumps. Moreover, in many cases, prices and economic activity have risen faster in the service sectors during booms than they have in the resource sectors; conversely, the slump in services during downturns – falling commercial and residential real-estate values and rising foreclosures -has often been more severe than the contraction in the resource sectors that is brought about by falling prices.

The distinctive features of a regional economy perhaps make the application of general-equilibrium models even more pertinent. Two basic features of a regional economy distinguish it from a national economy. The first is that a regional economy is far more "open" on the factor supply side, especially with regard to its labor market. A variety of studies have shown that interprovincial migration and, hence, provincial labour supplies are

---

23. See Whalley and Trela, *Regional Aspects of Confederation*, and William G. Watson, "The Regional Consequences of Free(r) Trade with the United States," in *Still Living Together*, ed. Coffey and Polese.

24. Norrie and Percy, *Energy Price Increases, Economic Rents and Industrial Structure*.

sensitive to differences in real income between provinces.[25] The second distinguishing feature is that, because provinces have no control over monetary policy or exchange rates, regional economies must function without this important mechanism of adjustment to balance-of-payments shocks. These two factors together tend to reinforce the important role of service-sector prices in accommodating the impact of booming (or contracting) resource sectors and contribute to the instability inherent in the impact of booming resource sectors on regional growth.

In a national economy, the labor supply can realistically be treated as fixed, with the result that much of the adjustment to economic shocks comes about through a reallocation of labor among competing sectors. A regional economy, on the other hand, since it can draw upon labor supplies from the rest of the country, should experience less of the "squeezing" of industrial structure that results from sectoral competition for labor. But because interregional labor markets respond to incentives for interprovincial migration only with a lag, the effect of intersectoral reallocation of labor, in the short run at least, is still significant. More important, the longer-term response to regional shocks – interprovincial migration – generates significant shifts in the structure of demand. Its impact on the demand for population-sensitive capital formation is dramatic. Booming resource sectors can initiate large inflows of migrants and consequently, large increases in the demand for housing and commercial fixed-capital formation. Thus, prices in these nontraded sectors may rise significantly, enabling them to bid labor away from other sectors whose output prices are set externally. Moreover, since nontraded prices are also inputs in most sectors, their increase places upward pressure on the regional cost structure. Historically, all booms in the West have been associated with a rapid rise in urban and rural land prices, and all slumps, with an equally rapid fall.

Service-sector prices also play an important role in a regional economy's adjustments to terms of trade, or supply-side shocks. The ratio of traded to nontraded prices – the relative price of tradeables -is often referred to in the international trade literature as the "real" exchange rate. At the regional level, the movement in the real exchange rate depends on the relative importance of income effects and intersectoral shifts in labor. At the provincial level in Canada, the sharp rise in nontraded prices that often accompanies booming sectors is the equivalent of an appreciation of the region's implicit exchange rate. The crowding-out of both the nonbooming

25. See S. L. Winer and D. Gauthier, *International Migration and Fiscal Structure* (Ottawa: Economic Council of Canada, 1982), and K. E. Mills, M. B. Percy, and L. S. Wilson, "The Influence of Fiscal Incentives on Interregional Migration: Canada, 1961-78," *Canadian Journal of Regional Science* 6 (1983): 207-230.

export sectors and the import-competing sectors that is brought about by the rise in the real exchange rate helps reduce any net trade surplus the region is running, while in the longer term, wealth effects come into play to help achieve balance-of-payments equilibrium.

The key role of nontraded prices at the regional level rests in ensuring that relative prices within the region move in a direction that leads to a new balance-of-payments equilibrium. While national economies can use exchange-rate policies to accommodate balance-of-payments shocks, regional economies must rely on automatic market mechanisms, such as movements in the so-called real exchange rate.

One reason that so many resource-based national economies found themselves worse off at the end of the boom is that the crowding-out accompanying booming sectors had disastrous consequences for the competitive position of traditional export and import-competing sectors. In terms of employment and production, these sectors declined in relative and, in many cases, absolute, size. The end of the resource boom was then accompanied by a painful and costly reallocation of economic activity, as sectors of former strength responded slowly to the incentives to expand. The crowding-out accompanying the booming sectors led some economies to run large balance-of-payments deficits even when resource prices were still rising, let alone when they began to fall.

At the regional level, the nature of the economic adjustments accompanying booming sectors also meant significant crowding-out of traditional export and import-competing sectors **and** large movements in the real exchange rate, the relative price of tradeables. The volatility in the economic environment that accompanied these shifts in industrial structure and relative prices meant a high degree of economic instability, especially in regions such as Alberta. It is not surprising that economic diversification became such a pressing issue throughout the 1970s in the province – all the forces of adjustment promoted greater specialization.

Economic Adjustment and Its Implications for Aggregate and Per-capita Income

In the regional context, the various models that we have discussed share a common feature: when properly specified, they all highlight the critical importance of distinguishing between short- and long-run adjustments to economic shocks. The short-run is the period during which the capital stock can be treated as fixed at the industry level, and the supply of labor as fixed to the region, but mobile among sectors. In the short run, much of the adjustment to economic shocks takes the form of movements in prices, especially nontraded ones, and in the returns to labor, land, and capital.

For a small region, it is quite possible that real per-capita income could diverge significantly from that of the larger national economy. In the longer term, however, differences in rates of return to capital lead to changes in the capital stock, until returns across regions and countries are equal, subject to the presence of risk premiums. Furthermore, differences in real wages will induce interregional migration, until there remains no economic return to subsequent migration. In the long run, a small regional economy faces highly responsive supplies of labor and capital. Short-term variations in factor returns act as a signal for entry or exit in the longer term. Regional economies can be viewed as "price-adjusters" (especially in the markets for capital and labor) in the short run, and as "quantity-adjusters" in the long run.

Certainly Alberta has many of the attributes of a small, open economy of the type discussed above. The provincial labor market is small relative to that of the rest of Canada, and the evidence suggests that interprovincial migration is responsive to real-wage differentials. There is absolutely no doubt that the province is a price-taker in capital markets and can draw upon funds from the rest of Canada and the world without influencing the price of capital. In most export and import-competing goods markets, the region is effectively a price-taker, either through the outcome of market forces or as a result of federal government fiat.

This perspective of Alberta has some gloomy implications, at least with regard to the ability of provincial policy makers to affect provincial per-capita incomes in the long run. The mobility of labor and capital among provinces means that in the long run, the provincial economy faces an essentially externally set ratio of cost of labor to cost of capital. Consequently, it is very difficult for the province to increase per-capita income permanently, relative to other regions. Provincial policies may influence real per-capita incomes in the short run but, as factor markets respond, the net effect will be reflected mainly as a change in the **amount** of capital and labor in the province, not in their economic returns.

Possible Causal Factors

It is readily apparent from the foregoing that, contrary to common perception, the determinants of the performance and structural characteristics of a small, resource-based, open economy such as Alberta's are both numerous and complex. As a result, it is no simple matter to isolate and quantify all of the factors contributing to the province's economic reversal and, in the post-1985 period, to its apparent strength in adversity. Nevertheless, the body of theory does provide some valuable direction for separating causes and effects and for identifying possible causal factors.

Specifically, it points to the following as potentially significant causes:

1. shifts in resource prices and policies or in external resource demands that produce changes in the performance of the province's basic industries and, consequently, in the overall performance of the Alberta economy;

2. shifts in the exogenous factors (interest rates, policy decisions regarding economic growth in regions that purchase Alberta's exports, etc.) that affect overall levels of investment and government expenditure in the province, as well as the level of provincial exports;

3. general shifts in Alberta's terms of trade and trade balances, as well as in provincial fiscal balances and in the regional distribution of federal fiscal balances.

It is useful to note that various avenues of adjustment associated with these causal factors are important in determining both the responses within the provincial economy and the net economic consequences. As indicated earlier, these include adjustments involving interregional migration, multiplier and accelerator processes, sector-specific price and wage changes, and various automatic stabilizers operating through imports, taxes, and fiscal transfers.

Explanations of Alberta's Economic Downturn

Given the abundance of theories and the scarcity of empirical work on the topic, it is not surprising that there are many popular – though not necessarily valid – explanations for Alberta's dramatic and prolonged economic downturn in the early 1980s. These typically place the blame on one, or some combination, of the following: high interest rates; falling resource prices; changed expectations with respect to future energy prices; inappropriate government policies, especially those concerning oil and gas; and the inevitability of a bust at the end of every boom. In this section, we shall summarize the results of various analyses of the downturn in an attempt at least to reduce the list to those explanations that are consistent with the theories outlined previously, as well as with the available data.

In his analysis of the causes of diverging regional economic performances in Canada, Edward Carmichael examined the role of energy prices and policies, nonenergy commodity prices, macroeconomic policies (including the fiscal-monetary mix and federal-provincial fiscal policies), and trade and investment policies.[26] He generally employed a five-region

---

26. Edward A. Carmichael, *New Stresses on Confederation: Diverging Regional Economies*, Observation no. 28 (Toronto: C. D. Howe Institute, 1986).

breakdown (Atlantic Canada, Quebec, Ontario, the Prairies, and British Columbia); hence not all of his results can be related specifically to Alberta. Nevertheless, it is reasonable to expect that many of his conclusions regarding the performance of the Western Canadian economy are generally applicable to Alberta.

Based on his analysis of changes over the period 1980-85, Carmichael concluded that external factors (low international prices for agricultural and forest products, minerals, and petroleum) were the dominant causes of the poor performance of the Western Canadian economy and of the serious regional imbalances in economic activity across the country. He also noted that "rather than providing a stabilizing influence, key government policies have actually aggravated differences in regional performance." For example, "the impact of federal monetary and fiscal policies on real interest rates and the external value of the Canadian dollar has created greater problems for the resource-producing provinces of the West and the Atlantic region than for Central Canada."[27] Further, he concluded that trade and industrial policies (such as the Voluntary Export Restraint Agreement and various federal and provincial industrial subsidies) "have favored Ontario and Quebec, while the energy pricing and taxation have weakened economic activity in Western Canada."[28]

Another diagnosis of Alberta's economic downturn is contained in the expert evidence provided by Scarfe, Harries, and others to the Estey Commission, and is summarized in the commission's final report.[29] Included here is an extensive examination of the potential causes of the downturn (such as interest rates, poor decision making by firms, energy and other commodity prices, changes in expectations, shifts in exports and in the province's terms of trade, and the National Energy Program [NEP]), as well as of the timing and reasons for the decisions to cancel energy and other key investments in Alberta. The commission's general conclusion was that the initiating factor was the NEP, the effects of which were compounded by high interest rates, and later, in 1986, by a deterioration in Alberta's terms of trade.[30]

In this regard, it is useful to recall that, by 1980, investment had become the primary engine of growth in Alberta (see pp. 15). Thus, the exodus of an

---

27. Ibid., p. 18.

28. Ibid., p. 19.

29. See Hon. Willard Z. Estey, *Report of the Inquiry into the Collapse of the CCB and Northland Bank* (Ottawa: Supply and Services, 1986). The expert evidence of Scarfe, Harries, and others, as well as evidence arising from cross-examination, can be found in the transcripts for the Estey Inquiry.

30. Ibid., p. 72.

estimated $11.5 billion in investment expenditures caused by the NEP set in motion a negative multiplier-accelerator process that, by 1982, had spread the effects to almost every component of the provincial economy.

It is also interesting to note in this context that the evidence presented to the Estey Commission contradicts some of the more popular explanations of the collapse of the Alberta economy: for example, that it was due to a decline in agricultural or energy prices and production. As shown in Figures 13 to 15, farm receipts remained fairly stable over this period; the gross revenue from the sale of oil, natural gas, and byproducts increased at a healthy rate; and the average prices received for oil and gas did not fall until 1986. Also, the province's trade balance steadily improved right up to the end of 1985 (see Figure 10), Alberta's terms of trade did not deteriorate until 1986 (see Figure 16) and the total value of Alberta exports generally increased until 1985 (see Figure 17).

Another factor frequently cited as contributing to the downturn is the change in expectations with respect to future oil and gas prices. As shown in Figure 18, the average price for domestic conventional crude oil was held well below the international price until 1985 and, although the international price dipped between 1981 and 1983, the domestic price continued to increase throughout the period to 1985. It has been argued, however, that price expectations were based more on the international price than on the domestic price. Consequently, according to this view, it was the dip in the international price and the resulting change in expectations, rather than the NEP, that accounted for the sharp drop in energy investment and economic activity in Alberta.[31] Indeed, the evidence presented to the Estey Commission indicates that this was a significant factor in the cancellation of several planned energy megaprojects. It does not, however, seem to be able to explain the large drop in investment in exploration and development drilling between 1980 and 1983. Canadian and U.S. firms would presumably have been subject to the same changes in expectations regarding energy prices (and interest rates), yet the trends in energy investment diverged sharply in the two countries. Just before the introduction of the NEP, there were about 550 active drilling rigs in Western Canada, compared with roughly 2,100 in the United States. Immediately following the NEP, the number of active rigs in Western Canada declined rapidly (to about 120 by 1982), while the number in the United States increased dramatically (to about

---

31. For example, by 1981, exploration expenditures had dropped 20 percent from their 1980 level and, by 1982 they were just over 50 percent of their 1980 level. (Statistics Canada, Cat. nos. 61-205 and 61-206, and the Canadian Petroleum Association, *Statistical Handbook*, section 4, table 3B.

Figure 13. Cash Receipts from Farming Operations, Alberta

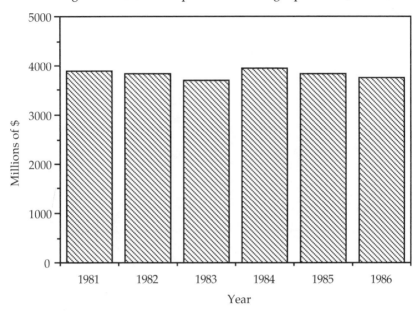

Source: Statistics Canada (21-001 and 21-603).

Figure 14. Value of Oil, Natural Gas and By-Product Production, Alberta

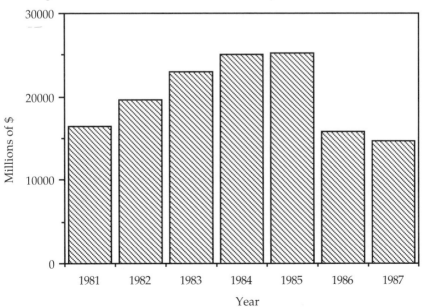

Source: Statistics Canada (26-201).

Figure 15. Average Prices for Alberta Oil and Gas

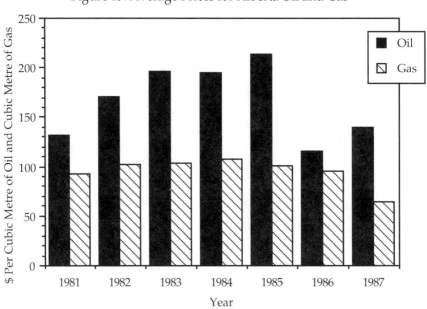

Source: Alberta Bureau of Statistics (ASIST – 6227 and 6228).

Figure 16. Price Indexes for Alberta Exports and Imports

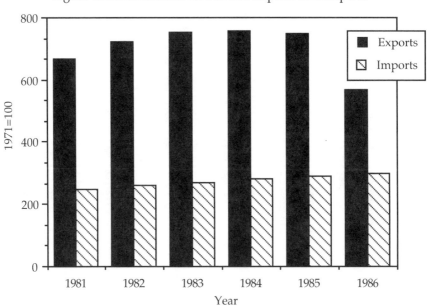

Source: Statistics Canada (26-201).

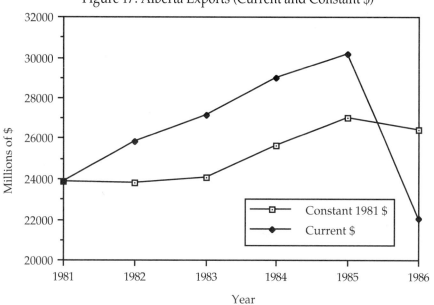

Figure 17. Alberta Exports (Current and Constant $)

Source: Alberta Bureau of Statistics, Alberta Economic Accounts.

4,300 by 1982).[32] Thus, it is reasonable to conclude that, if the change in price expectations (and high interest rates) was a factor in the collapse of energy investment in the province, it was certainly much less important than the NEP.

In an attempt to independently test the factors highlighted in the diagnoses summarized above, and to evaluate several others, we performed a number of simulations using MAE (Model of the Alberta Economy: Version 2.0). This is a 1,200-equation econometric model of the Alberta economy similar in design to CANDIDE; it incorporates most of the driving forces, linkages, and adjustments outlined thus far.[33] The basic procedure involved a comparison of actual (historical) performance with that predicted by the model under various "what if" conditions pertaining to energy prices and policies, interest-rate levels, fiscal policies, agricultural and other commodity prices, and so on.

---

32. Data provided by Robert McRae and John Helliwell (from the MACE data bank, University of British Columbia).

33. This model is described in Robert L. Mansell and A. S. Kwaczek, *Model of the Alberta Economy, MAE 2.0*, Project Papers, vols. 1-10 (Calgary: University of Calgary, 1980). For a summary of the model and the main linkages, see Robert L. Mansell, A. S. Kwaczek, and W. Kerr, "An Econometric Model of the Alberta Agricultural Sector," *Western Economic Review* 3, no. 4 (1985): 7-24.

Figure 18. Average International and Domestic Crude Oil Prices, 1971-1987
(in Canadian dollars per cubic metre)

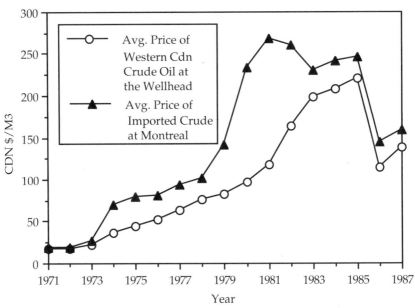

Source: Data from Canadian Petroleum Association, Statistical Handbook (Section
IV, Tables 1 and 3).

It is important to emphasize that, while this approach is useful in
establishing the general role of various factors in Alberta's economic
downturn, it cannot provide a definitive accounting of the situation. Ten
counterfactual cases were analyzed, but the number of combinations and
permutations that would in fact have to be considered to obtain a complete
accounting is immense. Moreover, certain elements, such as expectations, are
often elusive and certainly difficult to quantify. For these reasons, the results
presented here should be viewed as indicative rather than precise and
definitive.

The main conclusions of this analysis are as follows:

1.   By 1980, the Alberta economy had become highly vulnerable to any changes
     that would adversely affect investment expenditures. As noted earlier, the
     economy had come to be driven almost exclusively by investment, the most
     variable component of GDP. One consequence of this phenomenon was a
     construction sector considerably larger than what would normally be
     associated with a stable or steady-state growth path. In addition, it would
     appear that most of the expansion in the other nonresource sectors was

increasingly tied to the Keynesian, Leontief, and population multiplier effects (see pp. 24) arising from energy and energy-related investment expenditures. Consequently, any significant declines in this investment would have far larger negative impacts on the overall economy than they would otherwise have had.

2. Consistent with the conclusions of the Estey Commission, it appears that the NEP was the key factor in initiating the downturn, and its negative effects were compounded by the accompanying high interest rates. In this context, it might be noted that the preceding period of rapid growth, the debt-financed investment to accommodate it, and the debt-equity ratios in the energy sector (which were considerably higher than they would have been if – in the absence of regulated pricing and special energy taxes – more of the expansion had been financed out of cash flow) all served to magnify the effects of the high interest rates. Nevertheless, it is interesting to note that the simulation results show that, even with the high interest rates that produced serious recessions in other regions (and with energy investment trends comparable to those experienced in the United States over this period), but **without** the NEP, the Alberta economy would not have slid into recession during the 1981-85 period – that is, its growth rate would have been significantly reduced, but would have remained positive. In this case, however, the downturn following the collapse of oil and grain prices in 1986 would have been somewhat more severe, since many of the adjustments that took place in the 1981-85 period would have been concentrated within the 1986 and 1987 period.

3. Between 1980 and 1985, changes in resource prices, in the gross revenues of the agricultural and energy sectors, and in the province's terms of trade were generally positive factors and do not hold much explanatory power regarding Alberta's severe and prolonged economic downturn in this period.

4. The provincial government's fiscal stance was also a positive factor. As shown in Figure 19, its expenditures rose sharply from 1981 to 1983 as the economy faltered and the budget balance moved from a surplus of $1 billion in 1980 to a deficit of about $3 billion in 1983.[34]

---

34. Here, the comparison is between expenditures and revenues, excluding transfers of investment income from the Alberta Heritage Savings Trust Fund (AHSTF). Since the latter revenue item does not entail a drain on Alberta economic activity, it should generally be excluded in assessing the degree of net stimulation or restraint in the government's fiscal stance. In this assessment, it is also necessary to distinguish between actual-and-full employment surpluses and deficits.

Figure 19. Government of Alberta Revenues, Expenditures and Fiscal Balances, 1980-1987

(in billions of dollars and for fiscal years beginning in the years shown)

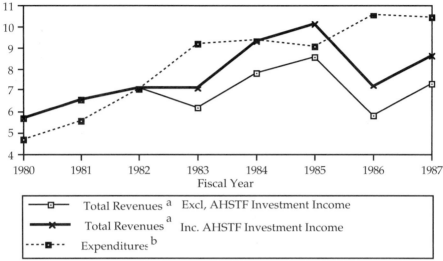

| | Total Revenues [a] Excl, AHSTF Investment Income |
| Total Revenues [a] Inc. AHSTF Investment Income |
| Expenditures [b] |

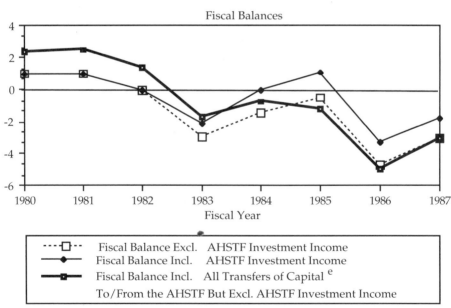

Fiscal Balances

Fiscal Balance Excl. AHSTF Investment Income
Fiscal Balance Incl. AHSTF Investment Income
Fiscal Balance Incl. All Transfers of Capital [e]
To/From the AHSTF But Excl. AHSTF Investment Income

Source: Alberta Treasury, Financial Summary and Budgetary Review, various years.

Notes: a. Total revenues are net of tax expenditures on the non-renewable resource sector.

b. Total budgetary expenditures plus voted and statutory appropriations.

c. That is, all transfers of non-renewable resource revenue to the AHSTF from the General Revenue Account and transfers to the General Revenue Account from the disposal of AHSTF assets are incorporated.

5. The federal government has consistently run large fiscal surpluses with
    Alberta,[35] producing a strong fiscal drag on the provincial economy. As
    indicated in Figure 20 and in the fiscal balances set out in Appendix A, these
    surpluses were particularly large during the NEP era and demonstrate
    another mechanism through which energy policies have served to transfer
    income and economic activity out of the province. Because of such policies,
    (involving special taxes and low levels of federal spending), Alberta has
    continued to be the only province with which the federal government runs a
    fiscal surplus -indeed, until 1983, this surplus was sufficiently large to more
    than offset the province's positive trade balance. Nevertheless, Carmichael
    has argued that these federal fiscal surpluses with Alberta are consistent
    with effective stabilization; that is, as a percentage of Alberta GDP, the
    federal fiscal surplus declined over the period 1981-84, as the economy
    weakened.[36] This argument is no doubt valid in the narrow sense that the
    deflationary impacts of federal tax and expenditure policies on Alberta's
    economy became less pronounced. But the simulations indicate that not only
    the direction of change, but also the size and sign of the fiscal balance are
    important. First, the results show that, in the absence of a continued rapid
    escalation in energy prices and energy investment, the exceedingly large
    federal fiscal surpluses with Alberta as early as the mid-1970s began to exert
    substantial deflationary effects on the provincial economy. In other words,
    in the model, the size of these surpluses, combined with any levelling of
    investment expenditures, is sufficient to generate a major recession. Second,
    the simulations demonstrate that in light of the collapse of investment that
    actually occurred and the associated negative multiplier effects, a rapid
    switch from a fiscal surplus to a fiscal deficit (of at least $2 billion annually)
    would have been required to keep Alberta's economic performance in line
    with the Canadian average during the 1982-84 period. Third, the simulations
    show that most of the stabilization effects associated with the provincial
    government's increase in expenditures and move to a fiscal deficit were
    negated or offset by the federal government's fiscal surplus. Finally, as noted
    by Carmichael, from the perspective of overall regional stabilization in
    Canada, it is difficult to justify stimulative federal fiscal deficits with regions
    experiencing rapid growth (such as Ontario) and, at the same time,

---

35. As mentioned earlier, the federal fiscal balance for a region is defined as the difference
    between total federal revenues collected in the region and total federal expenditures
    returned to it (in the form of transfers and expenditures on goods and services). A surplus
    indicates that federal tax and expenditure policies, taken together, operate to deflate the
    regional economy, while a deficit indicates a net injection or stimulus to the regional
    economy.

36. Carmichael, *New Stresses on Confederation*, p. 15.

Figure 20. Net Federal Fiscal Balances and Trade Balances for Alberta and Ontario, 1975-1985

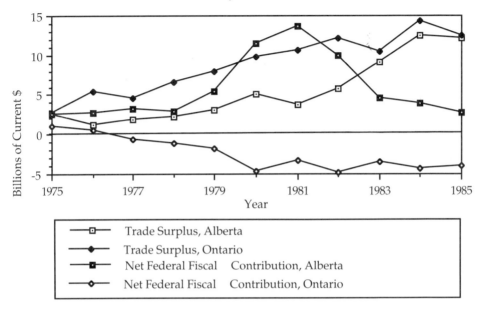

Combined Effects of Trade and Federal Fiscal Balances on Regional Aggregate Demand

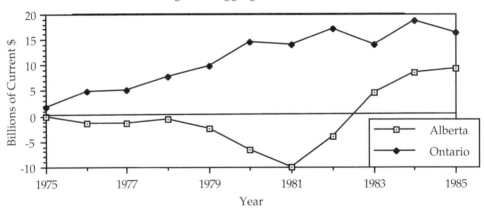

Source: Table 4 of Mansell and Schlenker, "An Analysis of the Regional Distribution of Federal Fiscal Balances."

deflationary fiscal surpluses with Alberta, a province with a weak and faltering economy.[37]

6. The simulations also reveal that the effects of the factors outlined above were compounded by the large migrations of people out of the province (see Figure 5). These outflows created substantial excess capacity in housing and other infrastructure, which contributed greatly to declines in investment and construction employment.[38] It is evident that there were also significant negative consequences for employment and income in a number of other important industries, especially food and beverages and retail trade. Although modest shifts in migration and population growth are appropriate adjustments in response to secular change in relative regional economic fortunes, very large swings of the type experienced by Alberta (for example, from a net inflow of 70,800 in 1981-82 to a net outflow of 55,900 in 1983-84) are destabilizing and inefficient. Moreover, when the burden of adjustment to preventable short-run swings in regional economic activity is placed on interregional migration, large social costs are incurred, and the approach amounts to little more than a poorly disguised "guest worker" policy.

Summary

Our main objective in this section has been to explain the serious economic downturn experienced in Alberta between 1981 and 1984. By way of background, we noted that the province's weak economic performance since 1981 represented a significant departure from its average performance over the preceding two decades. In addition, the recession was unusually severe and lengthy compared with the recessions experienced by other regions, as well as with the province's earlier downturns. For example, the downturn that followed the energy boom of the late 1940s and early 1950s was mild, and the provincial economy continued to grow at a healthy rate over extended periods when real energy prices were in decline.

Several changes in the structure of the Alberta economy were also noted. Specifically, during the 1970s, investment had become the dominant engine of growth, and expansion in the nonresource sectors had become even more closely tied to energy and energy-related investment. And because investment is the most variable component of GDP, this meant that the economy became more and more vulnerable to factors that could

---

37. Ibid., p. 23.

38. For example, between 1981 and 1985, employment in the Alberta construction sector fell from 122 thousand to 68 thousand (Statistics Canada, Cat. no. 71-001).

significantly affect investment decisions, such as high interest rates or unfavorable energy policies.

Based on our review of the staple theory, export-base models, the Keynesian framework, and various general-equilibrium models, we isolated various potential causes of the province's economic downturn (and of its better-than-expected economic performance after the 1986 collapse of oil and grain prices). These included;

1.   shifts in resource prices and policies;

2.   changes in interest rates, in growth in other regions, and in expectations with respect to future commodity prices;

3.   general shifts in Alberta's terms of trade and trade balances; and

4.   changes in provincial fiscal policy and in the regional impacts of federal tax and expenditure policies.

Drawing upon this list of potential causes and the rather limited amount of empirical research available, we considered various explanations for the dramatic and prolonged economic downturn. One such explanation points to low international resource prices as the main cause, combined with federal monetary and fiscal policies that were particularly unfavorable for the resource-producing regions – policies leading to high interest rates and an appreciation of the Canadian dollar, as well as energy pricing and taxation regimes that weakened economic activity in Western Canada. Another analysis, related specifically to Alberta (as apposed to Western Canada), concludes that the National Energy Program was the initiating factor, and that its effects were compounded by high interest rates, followed, in 1986, by a deterioration of the province's terms of trade.

Finally, based on comparisons between actual performance and performance as predicted by an econometric model using various "what if" or counter factual conditions, we attempted to test the potential explanations suggested by the theory. Our analysis points to the need for a more complex explanation, but the key causal factors that nonetheless emerge are the National Energy Program, high interest rates, and unusually large net federal fiscal withdrawals from Alberta. The effects of these were, in turn, shown to be magnified by the structural changes produced by the preceding boom, the large negative multiplier-accelerator effects, and the substantial net out-migration from the province.

Notwithstanding certain differences in emphasis, all of these diagnoses place a significant portion of the blame on inappropriate or perverse government policies. Thus, although certain factors (such as the vagaries of externally determined commodity prices) are beyond effective control, it seems clear that considerable progress toward preventing the recurrence of such a severe and prolonged economic downturn in Alberta could be made through improved policy responses. We shall take this issue up again in Chapter 5.

3 Responses to Adversity

On the basis of its absolute level of performance, it is difficult to argue that, since 1981, the Alberta economy has been strong. For example, employment in the province did not return to the prerecession high of 1981 until May 1987 – compared with November 1983 for Ontario, March 1984 for the Atlantic region, June 1984 for Quebec, and May 1984 for Canada as a whole. In addition, relative to the national average, per-capita income has continued to fall. When this performance is considered in light of the severe adversities the province faced in the 1980s, however, a much different picture emerges: those adversities could have been expected to inflict far more damage than they did. The same holds for the dramatic declines in grain, oil, and gas prices that began in late 1985. Indeed, it is in the period following those declines that the strength of the provincial economy has become most evident. Although there has been no significant growth, neither has there been the dramatic reversal that was generally predicted predicted. Moreover, the downturn in the Alberta economy was shallower, and the recovery quicker than it was in Texas or Oklahoma (see Figure 8) – a sharp contrast to the 1981-84 period, when the situation was reversed.

There is no shortage of explanations for this apparent strength in adversity. One argument maintains that the economy is much more diversified than is commonly believed and that, as such, it is considerably less sensitive to swings in resource prices today than it was 10 or 20 years ago. Another suggests that, because of various lags, the full effects of the

1986 collapse of grain and oil prices has yet to be felt. Still others focus on the role of government policies vis-a-vis the agriculture and energy sectors and on the trickle-down effects of strong growth in the United States and central Canada.

Our objective in this chapter is to develop an explanation of Alberta's economic performance since the end of 1985 and, in doing so, to offer an assessment of these various hypotheses. Our general approach is the same as the one we employed in the previous chapter, and it is subject to all of the qualifications and cautions outlined there. In addition, because of complications arising due to a lack of current data and because the full effects of both policies and market adjustments will not be completely apparent for some years to come, our conclusions should once again be viewed as indicative rather than as precise and definitive.

Resource Sector Policies and Adjustments

The various simulations undertaken confirm that the resource sectors, especially agriculture and mining, remain the driving force in the Alberta economy. And, despite the dramatic drop in grain and energy prices, declines in employment and investment in these sectors were not nearly as sharp as might have been expected. In fact, in the 1986-87 period, employment in the agriculture sector rose by more than five thousand, and in the mineral-fuels sector, by slightly less than two thousand; there were also significant gains in the forestry sector and related industries (see Appendix B). It was therefore apparent that much of the strength of the economy must have derived from resource policies and adjustments that significantly reduced the downside in the sectors.

In the case of the agriculture sector, three main factors can be isolated. The first is the large increases in federal and provincial government injections since 1985, including the Special Grains Stabilization Program; write-downs of the Western Grain Stabilization Fund's deficit; injections to the Farm Credit Corporation; enhanced crop insurance; increased farm fuel subsidies; a feed-grain price adjustment; and a farm credit-stabilization program. In addition to those increased expenditures, grain production was somewhat higher than expected, and some input costs fell. Second, the livestock component of the industry has been particularly strong in recent years, partly as a result of low feed costs and partly because this period of low grain prices (associated with international subsidy battles) happened to correspond with the high point of livestock price cycles. The net result of such policies and adjustments and the diversification provided by the cattle, hog, dairy, and poultry industries has been a slight increase over 1985 levels in farm cash receipts and net farm income in 1986 and 1987[1] – and this is despite a drop of almost 50 percent in grain prices.

The shifts in policies and the market adjustments affecting the province's oil and gas industry have been equally significant. The main turning point in federal energy policy occurred with the election of the Conservative government in 1984. In March 1985, this government signed the so-called Western Accord with the governments of Alberta, Saskatchewan, and British Columbia. Under the agreement, which took effect on June 1, 1985, Canadian crude-oil prices, along with short-term exports of crude oil, were deregulated, and most of the special energy taxes and incentives under the NEP were either eliminated or phased out over a four-year period.[2] The other major policy shift occurred with the signing of the "Halloween Agreement,"[3] which provided for the deregulation of natural-gas pricing and markets. Other policy changes at the national level included the introduction of the Canadian Exploration, Development, and Incentive program (CEDIP)[4] and the National Energy Board's Market-Based Procedure, which replaced the surplus tests used to control gas exports.[5]

The Government of Alberta also instituted a variety of policies designed to stimulate the oil and gas industry. These included a phasing down of royalty rates, drilling-well servicing and geophysical incentives, and substantial injections via the Alberta Petroleum Incentives Program Fund, the Royalty Tax Credit program, and various royalty holidays. Taken together, these programs have, since 1985, provided injections to the industry of about $1 billion annually and have significantly lowered net royalty rates.[6] For example, the net royalty rate on gas (that is, the gross

1. Based on data from Statistics Canada, CANSIM Matrix nos. 3426 and 458 and Cat. no. 21-603.

2. Specifically, the Natural Gas and Gas Liquids Tax (NGGLT), the Canadian Ownership Surtax (COSC), the Petroleum Compensation Charge (PCC), and oil-export charges, along with federal subsidies on oil-transportation costs, were eliminated on June 2, 1985. The Petroleum Incentive Program (PIP) grants were terminated on March 31, 1986, and the Petroleum and Gas Revenue Tax (PGRT) was eliminated on all production coming on stream after April 1, 1985. For other production, the PGRT was to be phased out by January 1, 1989, but, with the collapse of oil prices, was eliminated in 1986 instead.

3. Officially titled the "Agreement Among the Governments of Canada, Alberta, British Columbia and Saskatchewan on Natural Gas Markets and Prices," October 31, 1985.

4. The CEDIP program was aimed mainly at smaller firms. It provided for grants of up to $3 million on the first $10 million of exploration and development expenditures.

5. For details, see National Energy Board, *Reason for Decision in the Matter of Review of National Gas Surplus Determination Procedures* (Ottawa: National Energy Board, July 1987).

6. For 1985 and 1986 alone, the total value of these programs was $1.9 billion (Alberta Treasury, *Financial Summary and Budget Review, 1985-86* [Edmonton: Alberta Treasury, 1986], schedule 7.

royalty rate, currently about 28.5 percent, net of various rebates and royalty holidays) is now slightly higher than 12 percent, compared with about 15 percent in the early 1970s. When all of these factors are taken together, the net backs to producers are now generally higher, even with the substantially lower prices, than they were in 1985.

Some elements of these policy shifts have been anything but stabilizing when viewed in the longer-run. For example, the deregulation of prices initiated in 1985, after prices and markets had been tightly regulated during the years of high international energy prices, left the industry completely exposed to the subsequent collapse of world oil prices. In retrospect, it could be argued that the timing was poor. But the very existence of the NEP, and the strident calls for further drops in gas prices by some of the consuming provinces, reveal an important asymmetry in national energy policy in Canada – namely, that it is appropriate to depress oil and gas prices artificially in order to generate large transfers to the net consuming provinces,[7] but inappropriate and unacceptable to slow down or reduce price declines in a falling market.

Nevertheless, other elements of these policy shifts did serve to cushion the industry from the full effects of the energy-price collapse; in particular:

1. While gross revenues from the sale of gas, gas byproducts, and oil fell by $9.4 billion between 1985 and 1986, royalty payments fell by $2.7 billion, and the elimination or reduction of a number of federal taxes offset a significant portion of this revenue decline.

2. The relaxation of restrictions on oil and gas exports allowed producers to increase production, especially for oil, and thereby offset part of the price decline (see Appendix Table C-1). In this regard, it is interesting to note that, since the expansion of the Interprovincial Pipe Line was completed, there has been no shut-in oil in Alberta. Also, as of the latter part of 1987, gas exports have increased substantially.

3. The elimination of the NEP has resulted in a substantial shift of exploration and development budgets back to Alberta. Because the new policy environment is not judged to be hostile (unlike the situation that prevailed under the NEP), and because of the lower royalty and tax rates, as well as

---

7. For example, from 1973 to 1985, transfers associated with regulated oil and gas pricing alone, from Alberta to Ontario, amounted to $34.6 billion (1987 dollars). From 1961 to 1972, when under the National Oil Program, prices for Alberta crude oil in Ontario were slightly above international levels, the associated net transfer from Ontario to Alberta amounted to just under $1.5 billion (1987 dollars). See Robert L. Mansell and R. Schlenker, "An Analysis of the Regional Distribution of Federal Fiscal Balances" (Working paper, University of Calgary, 1988).

greater potential and lower finding costs than are to be had in the mature producing areas of the United States, Alberta represents an attractive location for oil and gas investment, even at current price levels.

Complementing these policy changes have been a number of significant adjustments within the industry, including widespread consolidation and rationalization. As noted earlier, one of the effects of the NEP was the creation or expansion of many Canadian oil and gas companies via special incentives and a reliance on debt. With the removal of these incentives and the collapse of energy prices, many of these companies proved non-viable, particularly given their debt loads. The absorption of their assets by larger or more financially stable firms has undoubtedly resulted in an industry better able to survive short-run price fluctuations.

Another important component of this adjustment has been the substantial cost reductions achieved by the industry. For example, the cost per exploratory meter drilled was $441 in 1986, compared with $448 in 1981.[8] The reductions in the cost of producing synthetic crude oil from oil sands have been even more dramatic. In 1985, these costs for the Suncor facility at Fort McMurray were about $33 per barrel; by mid-1987, they had been brought down to $16 per barrel (similar reductions were also achieved at the Syncrude plant). Heavy-oil-production costs also dropped significantly.[9]

Finally, as in the case of agriculture, an element of intra-industry diversification has become apparent. During the period of rising energy prices, the highest returns were achieved in upstream activities (that is, finding and developing oil and gas reserves), while downstream activities (refining and marketing) generally produced low returns. When oil and gas prices fell, however, the situation was reversed, with the result that, for the companies with both upstream and downstream interests, losses were significantly reduced.[10]

In summary, when the effects of the policies and adjustments relating to Alberta's agriculture and mining sectors are combined, simulations using MAE 2.0 reveal that they account for well over half the discrepancy between

8. Canadian Petroleum Association, *Statistical Handbook 1988*, (table 1, sec. 4; table 5, sec. 1).

9. Figures taken from a speech by Miles Supple, executive vice-president of Lunar's oil-sands group, delivered at Fort McMurray, Alberta, September 18, 1987. Amoco reduced the cost of producing heavy oil from its Elk Point project from $10 per barrel to $5 per barrel (*Calgary Herald*, June 3, 1987, p. F9).

10. For example, the upstream component of the Western Canadian oil and gas industry saw a fall from profits $2.9 billion in 1985 to losses of $1.8 billion in 1986. The downstream component, on the other hand, saw profits increase from $215 million in 1985 to $805 million in 1986 (data from the 1986 survey by the Petroleum Monitoring Agency, Government of Canada).

the province's actual performance and that predicted by the model solely on the basis of the declines in oil, gas, and grain prices. We shall outline the factors that explain the balance of this discrepancy, or gap, in the following section.

Macroeconomic Policies, Performance, and Adjustments

As explained earlier, federal fiscal policies, taken as a whole, resulted in the transfer of substantial amounts of income, employment, and provincial-government revenue out of the Alberta economy. It is evident that this fiscal drag continued at least until 1985, but at a reduced rate (see Figure 20 and Appendix A). Based on some rather crude projections for 1986, it would appear that, while Alberta remains the only province for which federal tax and expenditure policies remove more than they return, the size of the surplus continues to shrink. While this situation can hardly be described as consistent with regional fairness or the goal of overall stabilization of the Alberta economy, it is nevertheless important to the extent that the degree of deflation associated with federal policies has been reduced.

As in the case of the other regions, the significant declines in interest rates, particularly in the latter part of 1986 and early 1987, appear to have had a significant positive impact on the Alberta economy. It has been the stimulative effects of the large provincial fiscal deficits, however, combined with the reductions in imports to Alberta, that have been the most significant macroeconomic factors contributing to Alberta's better-than-expected economic performance in recent years. While it could be argued that the substantial provincial tax increases that were introduced in the first half of 1987 hindered rather than helped Alberta's economic recovery, the fact remains that, since 1985, the provincial government has provided a net injection of well over $9 billion to the province's economy (see Figure 19) – by far the single most important factor contributing to its surprising performance and perhaps best evidenced by the strong growth in activities primarily financed by the government. For example, as shown in Appendix B, education and related services and health and welfare services were the only industries that had substantial employment gains in 1986 and 1987, as well as over the 1981-87 period as a whole.

The declines in the ratio of imports to GDP since 1981 (see Figure 9) helped to reduce the degree of leakage, and hence to stabilize the economy. These declines can in large part be attributed to the emergence of excess capacity in some investment-related industries and a generally low level of investment in the province since 1981.[11] But there is some evidence (presented in the next section) that they can also be attributed, in part, to the development and growth of import-replacing industries in Alberta.

With respect to regional balance-of-payments adjustments, some mention should also be made of the shifts that occurred in nonfiscal financial flows. Here the evidence is spotty, but it does suggest some important offsetting adjustments. On the one hand, there have been rather large decreases in chartered-bank lending the province.[12] Based on discussions with people in the real estate and securities business, however, these were likely more than offset by substantial inflows of equity funds, especially from Ontario and from the United States, Hong Kong, Switzerland, and Germany. For the most part, these inflows have been generated by the perception that the province's assets (such as commercial real estate, oil and gas reserves, gas plants, etc.) have been significantly undervalued and consequently represent an excellent investment opportunity.

Other potentially important macroeconomic factors include the behavior of saving rates, and various lags – that is, the apparent strength of the provincial economy could be related simply to consumers' drawing down their savings to finance expenditures or to similar lag effects in the behavior of business. Although a complete assessment of these factors is impossible until additional current data are available, they do not in general, appear to form an important part of the explanation. For example, the personal saving rate (that is, personal saving as a percentage of personal disposable income) in Alberta fell from 16.9 percent in 1985 to 14.3 percent in 1986. But this is not out of line with the situation nationally, where the rate declined from 15.4 percent in 1985 to 13 percent in 1986.[13] Nevertheless, it is interesting to note that, between the second quarter of 1986 and the second quarter of 1987, Alberta stood out as the province with the smallest increase in personal saving deposits held in chartered banks.[14]

---

11. The construction of various mega-projects prior to 1982, which involved imports of equipment that was not produced in the province, combined with the fact that many Alberta industries were already operating at capacity (meaning that additional inputs could be obtained only from sources outside the province), accounts in large part for the unusually high import-to-GDP ratios from the mid-1970s to 1981.

12. Between 1985 and the second quarter of 1987, total chartered-bank assets (loans, mortgages, etc.) in Alberta declined from $43.8 billion to $39.5 billion (Alberta Bureau of Statistics, ASIST Matrix no. 6256).

13. Based on data from Alberta Bureau of Statistics, ASIST Matrix nos. 6280 and 9578.

14. Statistics Canada, CANSIM Matrix no. B5518-30.

Market- and Policy-Induced Diversification

Based on the simulation results, it would appear that the factors outlined above (that is, resource-sector policies and adjustments, fiscal policies, macroeconomic adjustments, etc.) can account for between two-thirds and three-quarters of the gap between the actual performance of the Alberta economy in recent years and that predicted on the basis of shifts in resource prices only. The remainder must be attributable to structural changes within the economy, and here there are two (related) hypotheses. One suggests that a reversal of Dutch Disease, or market- induced diversification, is at play. That is, with the decline in wages and with other input costs associated with the weakening of the resource and construction sectors, many previously uneconomical manufacturing and service activities have become economical and attractive. The other maintains that the many policy initiatives by the provincial government to develop and diversify the economy have been effective, producing a more diversified economy that is less vulnerable to shifts in the fortunes of the agriculture and energy sectors.

It must be emphasized at the outset that it is extremely difficult to isolate the underlying causal factors and quantify the relative contributions of market forces and policy initiatives to these structural changes in the Alberta economy. In part, this is because employment creation in the province has shifted increasingly from large companies and megaprojects that are visible and easily identified to small firms and projects that are much less visible and easily lost in statistical aggregates.[15] For example, between 1978 and 1984, companies with less than five employees were responsible for 62 percent of the new jobs created in the province, and since 1982, very few jobs have been created by companies with more than 100 employees.[16] The problem of identifying and quantifying structural change is compounded by difficulties in establishing appropriate benchmarks. That is, it is important to distinguish between actual changes in employment in a particular industry and those that could have been expected given the industry's linkages to, say, oil and gas investment and the declines in this investment. In other words, the declines in employment in the majority of Alberta industries in

---

15. In this regard, it might be noted that shifts in the distribution of employment among broadly defined sectors such as manufacturing or services are virtually meaningless in terms of measuring structural change. For example, an intra-sectoral shift involving an expansion of electronics manufacturing and a decrease in manufacturing of products used as inputs to the oil and gas industry would clearly represent diversification away from the resource sector, but would not show up in aggregates for the manufacturing sector. Our attempts to use electrical-utility connection and disconnection data to isolate such intra-sectoral shifts proved unsuccessful because of discontinuities and inconsistencies between the classifications used by utilities and the Standard Industrial Classification (SIC) codes.

16. *Alberta Business*, October 1987, p. 15.

recent years (see Appendix B) often hide the fact that, in the absence of diversifying behavior, the decreases would have been greater.

Nevertheless, some general trends can be identified. Perhaps the most apparent is that, by most measures, the Alberta economy is considerably more mature and highly developed today than it was the even 10 or 20 years ago, and this alone has added an element of stability. Although the production and export of fabricated materials is still small in comparison to that of primary and crude materials, it has expanded significantly. The increased reliance on local sources for many fabricated and end products, particularly those used in construction (lumber, windows, fixtures, etc.) – and hence the lower propensity to import – has served to reduce the degree of leakage from the provincial economy. Also important are the favorable (regional) balance-of-payments effects resulting from reductions in interest-payment leakages from the province through the use of the Alberta Heritage Savings Trust Fund as a vehicle for providing debt financing for provincial crown corporations and municipalities. Furthermore, as noted by the Economic Council of Canada, the steady shift in employment from goods production to services has had an important stabilizing influence.[17] In general, the service sectors are less capital intensive and, as a consequence, a larger percentage of the payments to factor inputs remain in the region. Moreover, service sectors tend to be less vulnerable, at least in the short term, to swings in externally determined variables, such as commodity prices.

Another aspect of this development and increased maturity has been the substantial diversification that has taken place within many of the large Alberta-based corporations that form a key component of the province's economic base. Nova, An Alberta Corporation; Alberta Energy Company Ltd.; and ATCO Ltd. are but three examples of such companies. They have diversified not only in terms of their markets, but also in the terms of range of commodities they produce. In addition to their activities related to oil and gas, they have become heavily involved in areas such as petrochemicals, forestry and wood products, communications equipment, and various other types of manufacturing, all of which has helped to stabilize both this corporate base and the broader provincial economy.

One of the most visible elements of structural change, and the one that is most easily tied to the diversification initiatives of the provincial government, is the development and growth of the ethane-based petrochemical industry. Before the mid-1970s, almost all of the ethane derivable from Alberta's natural-gas resources was being lost in the gas streams leaving the province. The potential to recoup this lost value, the

---

17. Economic Council of Canada, *Western Transition*.

relatively high cost of crude oil-based petrochemical feedstocks, and
government assurances of security of supply and of reasonable terms for the
extraction of the ethane as stipulated in the Dowling Agreement, or "Letters
of Understanding," between the industry and the government provided the
incentives for the development of a world-scale petrochemical industry.[18]
This industry currently consists of seven ethane-extraction plants (three of
which rank as the largest in North America), two world-scale
ethylene-manufacturing plants, a variety of liquid-transportation and storage
facilities, and nine ethylene-derivative plants producing a wide variety of
resins and other primary petrochemicals. The industry directly employs
more than 6,000 people and currently generates about $1 billion annually in
export earnings. In recent years, many smaller operations have been added
to manufacture a range of plastic end products from the resins produced by
the industry, and further expansion of ethylene and derivative
manufacturing has been planned.[19]

The ethane-based petrochemical industry has unquestionably had an
important stabilizing effect on the Alberta economy. A sizable portion of the
roughly $5 billion (1987 dollars) in associated investment has occurred
during years when other investment in the province has been weak. The
industry has also added a substantial, and stable, market for natural-gas
producers. For example, the gas used for fuel and for shrinkage make-up
(that is, for replacing the BTUs lost from the gas stream leaving the province
when ethane is removed) now amounts, on an annual basis, to slightly less
than six percent of total Alberta gas sales, or about one-quarter of all gas
sales within the province. Unlike the situation in other markets, these fuel
and shrinkage-make-up sales do not vary significantly over the course of a
year or from year to year – that is, most of the adjustments are in prices
rather than levels of production. Consequently, the industry generates stable
employment and adds stability to the overall market for Alberta natural gas.
It is also interesting to note that the petrochemical industry is one of very few
manufacturing industries in the province to show an increase in employment
in the 1986-87 and 1982-87 periods (see Appendix B).

The development of the petrochemical industry and the diversification
undertaken by some of the large Alberta-based corporations have

---

18. It should be emphasized that this ethane-based industry developed alongside the province's
    already sizable petrochemical industry, which is based on the direct conversion of natural
    gas into products such as methanol and ammonia/urea. Data on the ethane-based
    petrochemical industry were obtained from various Industrial Development Permit
    applications to, as well as various interventions before, the Energy Resources Conservation
    Board (ERCB).

19. The latter includes a third ethylene-manufacturing plant and another polyethylene facility to
    be constructed by 1992.

significantly expanded and stabilized investment and exports. In terms of job creation, however, it is the less visible small-business sector that has played the dominant role in recent years, and it is here that the major portion of any market- or policy-induced diversification is likely to be found.

For all of the reasons outlined earlier, it is difficult to isolate and measure these shifts. Nevertheless, some general trends can be identified using data on business incorporations and industry employment (see Appendix B). One such trend is the significant growth of employment in the industry of services to business management,[20] particularly in 1986 and 1987. In fact, the increase of 8,200 jobs in this industry alone was almost sufficient to offset the loss of 8,700 jobs in the area of services incidental to mining during the course of these two years. Another trend involves a number of industries showing either slight increases in employment, or at least decreases that are smaller than would be expected, given the shifts in the agriculture and energy sectors. These include wood products; furniture and fixtures; printing, publishing, and allied products; electrical products; miscellaneous manufacturing; communications; amusement and recreation services; insurance and real estate; and personal services. The relative gains exhibited by these industries in the last few years are small on an individual-industry basis, but, taken together, they are significant. Furthermore, these induced shifts tend to be consistent with reports on the manner in which many individuals and small firms whose activities were previously tied exclusively to the energy sector have responded to adversity. For example, a survey by the Canadian Federation of Independent Business suggests that about two out of three of the small businesses that started up between 1978 and 1984 were initiated in response to a negative situation, such as the loss of a job, and that about two-thirds of the jobs created in recent years were generated by small business.[21] In this regard, it is interesting to note that, even in 1986, Alberta led all provinces in both rate of new business incorporations and the rate of new business incorporations adjusted for business failures (see Figure 21).[22] In any case, it would appear that the strong entrepreneurial drive

---

20. This industry includes the following: employment agencies and personnel services; computer services; security and investigation services; offices of accountants; advertising services; offices of architects; engineering and scientific services; offices of lawyers and notaries; offices of management and business consultants; and miscellaneous services to business management.

21. See *Alberta Business*, October 1987, p. 13.

22. It should be noted, however, that Alberta's lead in business incorporations was substantially greater in 1985, before the collapse of oil and grain prices, as well as in the years preceding the NEP. For example, in 1985, new business incorporations in the province rose by 16.3 percent over 1984 levels, and in 1980 they were up 35 percent over the 1979 levels (Alberta Department of Economic Development; data reported in the *Calgary Herald*, September 21, 1987, p. E5).

Figure 21. Per Capita Business Incorporations by Province, Average for 1986
(Ontario = 100)

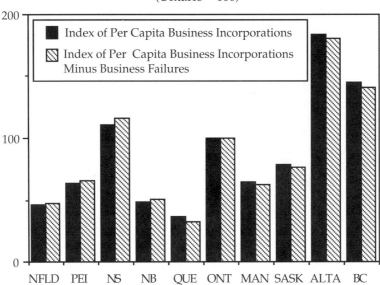

Source: Data on business incorporations and failures provided by Janet L. Welsh,
           Dunn and Bradstreet Canada Limited.

underlying these figures has been a significant factor contributing to the
province's resilience in face of adversity.

Such shifts in market-driven industries have been important both for
diversifying away from primary resources and for preventing the larger
reductions in employment that were expected in view of the magnitude of
the adversities. Nevertheless, the fact remains that by far the most significant
absolute employment growth in the province in recent years has been in
activities that are driven almost entirely by government expenditure. For
example, education and related services and health and welfare services
accounted for the bulk of the net job creation in 1986 and 1987 – a total of
19,500 new jobs (see Appendix B). Although, in many respects, this growth
represents an investment in future growth and diversification, it is
nonetheless heavily dependent on provincial government revenues that
remain highly vulnerable to downturns in the energy sector.

Although factors that account for the strength of the small-business
sector are difficult to quantify, it is clear that they are generally related to the
character of the province's economy and government policies. In many
respects, the character of the economy has been shaped historically by its
reliance on agriculture and petroleum. Both sectors are marked by

capital-intensive production processes, a high degree of risk, a large number of independent units, and exposure to the vagaries of international markets and government policies – all of which combine to preclude a strong base for organized labor and the kinds of values that are typically associated with a heavy concentration of labor-intensive industries. Rather, the foundation is rooted in rural-conservative values characterized by rugged individualism, risk taking, entrepreneurial awareness, and an appreciation of adversity, as well as of the ability adjust quickly to a volatile environment. These values, along with the requirements of an industrial base strongly oriented toward knowledge and technology (especially in the case of the energy sector and related industries), have worked to produce the most highly educated labor force in Canada.[23] Taken together, these characteristics define a very entrepreneurial, flexible, and mobile population, one that has strong incentives and abilities to respond to adversity by modifying existing business activities, and by creating new ones.

Provincial policies have also been important of encouraging and facilitating the growth and diversification of small-business enterprise. These policies have generally focused on maintaining low corporate tax rates and developing a wide variety of programs and agencies to assist in the start-up and financing of small businesses. Included among such programs and agencies are the Alberta Opportunity Company, the Agricultural Development Corporation, the Small Business Equity Corporations Program, Vencap Equities, the Alberta Stock Saving Plan, and regulatory changes allowing the creation of Junior Capital Pools. Although no attempt has been made to quantify the contributions of the many existing initiatives, evidence from other studies indicates that the focus of government policy on the financial aspects of small business has likely been a significant factor in Alberta's high rate of business formation.[24] In addition, the province has independently or, in several cases, in cooperation with the federal government, set up centers for research in microelectronics, medicine, oil-sands and enhanced oil recovery, coal mining, agriculture and food processing, and frontier engineering. While these research initiatives have

---

23. For example, the percentage of the adult population in each province with one or more university degrees is as follows: Alberta, 9.6 percent; Ontario, 9 percent; B.C., 8.2 percent; Manitoba, 7.4 percent; Nova Scotia, 7.4 percent; Quebec, 7.1 percent; Saskatchewan, 6.1 percent; PEI, 6.1 percent; New Brunswick, 6 percent; and Newfoundland, 4.7 percent. The linkage between high levels of education and the energy sector is supported by the fact that Calgary has by far the most highly educated population in the province and the nation. (Statistics Canada, *Labour Force Survey of Economic Regions, 1981* [Ottawa: Minister of Supply and Services, 1985].

24. See David G. Tims, "Capital Markets" (Unpublished manuscript, Western Centre for Economic Research, Edmonton, 1987).

already resulted in a number of new businesses, it will be many years before
their full effects can be fairly assessed.

Summary

It is evident that the Alberta economy is much more highly developed and
has a broader base than it did even 15 years ago. Furthermore, there have
been some notable shifts in the structure of the economy in recent years that
can account for a significant portion of the province's strong economic
performance after the dramatic declines in grain and energy prices. Of
particular importance here are the diversification undertaken by some of the
large Alberta-based companies (including the development of the
petrochemical industry) and the strong response of the small-business sector.
The latter appears to be related to market inducements (fewer opportunities
in the oil and gas and related industries, job-losses, and lower input costs),
the character of the labor force (highly skilled and highly educated, flexible,
entrepreneurial and risk taking, with a strong sense of rugged individualism
and self-reliance), and provincial government policies aimed at assisting new
business development.

Nevertheless, the economy's impressive performance is explained in
major part not by these structural shifts, but by government policies and
adjustments within the resource sectors. The substantial agricultural support
programs and the large reductions in energy taxes and royalties, in
combination with a partial recovery of oil prices, increases in energy
production, industry rationalization, and cost reductions, have played a key
role in stabilizing the economy. Also important have been the stimulative
effects of the large provincial fiscal deficits and the automatic stabilization
that accompanies reduced imports. Although federal tax and expenditure
policies taken together have continued to produce a net leakage of activity
and income from Alberta (while at the same time providing a net stimulus to
the other provincial economies), the size of this fiscal drag has been
significantly reduced. As a package, these changes in resource and overall
fiscal policies, the macroeconomic adjustments, and the adjustments made
by the agriculture and energy sectors account for two-thirds to three-quarters
of the gap between Alberta's actual economic performance in the last few
years and that predicted solely on the basis of the drop in grain and energy
prices. This is not to suggest that the types of market- and policy-induced
development and diversification evident in Alberta are unimportant. Indeed,
there is considerable evidence to suggest that they have added substantially
to the strength and stability of the economy. Moreover, they amply
demonstrate the importance of pursuing policies that facilitate rather than

hinder adjustments or shifts in the economic environment. As with any type of structural change, however, market- and policy-induced diversification is very much a long-run process that requires decades rather than years for its stabilizing effects to become readily apparent. As such, it is unreasonable to expect this kind of diversification, no matter how successful or rapid it is, to offset the effects of swings in the province's agriculture and energy sectors (which remain the economy's key driving forces) or to act as a substitute for policies aimed at stabilizing these sectors and the overall economy.

Before we explore these policy issues, it is necessary to broaden our analytical perspective. For example, the results we have presented thus far apply only to the post-1980 period, and it is not clear that the sources of instability identified for this period are relevant in the longer run or that the degree of Alberta's instability is more serious than that experienced by other provinces. These issues are taken up in the following chapter.

4 | Degree and Sources of Instability

The variability and vulnerability demonstrated by the Alberta economy during the 1980s have understandably had to strident demands for policies aimed at increasing stability. These economic difficulties by themselves, however, do not enable us to establish the degree of the problem, its fundamental causes, or the appropriate policy responses. It is particularly important to determine whether the recent variability is an isolated event arising out of circumstances that are unlikely to be repeated or part of a long-run pattern of inherent instability. Moreover, since all regional economies are subject to swings, the key issue is not so much the absolute degree of variability within the Alberta economy, but the severity of the problem when measured against the economic fluctuations in other Canadian regions.

In this chapter, we begin with a brief discussion of the various types and measurements of instability, and proceed to some regional comparisons and an evaluation of the factors underlying the variability in the Alberta economy. Finally, we present some general observations about the direction and the strengths and vulnerabilities of the provincial economy, to provide a backdrop to the subsequent discussion of policy alternatives.

Defining and Measuring Economic Instability

In a purely statistical sense, instability is a fairly simple concept. Specifically, it refers to the degree of variation that occurs relative to a given benchmark (usually, the mean of the variable). In the context of a regional economy, however, there are additional dimensions that add complexity to both the definition and the measurement of instability. For example, there is a temporal dimension that makes it necessary to distinguish among seasonal, cyclical, and secular instabilities. Furthermore, it is necessary to take into account that there is no simple relationship between variability and economic costs and, indeed, that only certain types of instability have adverse consequences. In other words, to the extent that variations are predictable, there can, in some instances, be accommodating changes in the behavior of individuals and firms that can completely or partially offset any existing economic costs. In light of these complications, it is useful to begin with a brief discussion of the meanings and measurement of regional economic instability.

The Temporal Dimension

From a temporal perspective, there are four main types of regional economic instability: seasonal, cyclical, secular, and "random" instability. Seasonal instability refers to the fluctuations that regularly occur over the course of a year and that are tied to seasonal changes in the climate or to various conventional/institutional factors, such as holidays. Variations associated with the business cycle or the cycles in, say, resource prices comprise cyclical instability, while secular instability refers to the long-term decline of one or more elements of the region's economic base (the eventual exhaustion of Alberta's conventional oil and gas resources would be an example of the latter). Finally, random instability refers to variations in prices or markets resulting from seemingly random, or unpredictable, events, such as an outbreak of war or a disruption of international trade.

Unfortunately, it is not always easy to determine which type of variability is at issue in policy discussions regarding Alberta's "instability problem." During the 1970s, when the fear of energy shortages was widespread, discussions tended to focus on secular instability. The main concern seemed to be that the province's economic base would rapidly decline as its conventional oil and gas resources became depleted. But, with the general cyclical downturn in resource prices and the various random shocks that occurred during the 1980s (such as OPEC's over-production in 1986 and the outbreak of the agriculture- subsidization wars), attention shifted to cyclical instability. What is perhaps most evident from this

experience is that the province has suffered from more than one type of
instability. And since policies for reducing, say, cyclical variability would
generally differ from those aimed at decreasing secular or seasonal
instability, this would in turn suggest the need for multidimensional
stabilization policies.

For analytical purposes, our focus here is on cyclical instability in the
Alberta economy. The reasons for this emphasis are as follows. First, while
seasonal variations do remain, to some extent, a problem,[1] it is the much
larger cyclical and random swings that tend to be the dominant concern in
discussions about the need for diversification. Second, although there may be
valid reasons to worry about the long-term decline of certain components of
the agricultural sector,[2] the experience gained over the last decade or so has
significantly reduced fears of a secular decline in Alberta's oil and gas
industry. It is now recognized that in the long run, energy prices are a much
more important factor affecting the province's oil and gas reserves and
production than is the physical exhaustion of conventional reserves. With
gradually increasing energy prices, the long-term potential for enhanced oil
recovery, as well as for heavy-oil and oil-sands development, is substantial.[3]
Furthermore, the point at which gas-reserve additions per unit of exploration
effort start to decline significantly has yet to be reached,[4] and, with rising
prices, synthetic gas derived from the province's abundant coal resources
represents an alternative source of gas over the long term. In short, declining
(real) energy prices, which would make the exploitation of Alberta's oil and

---

1. Although there has been a long run decline in the degree of seasonal instability in Alberta
    and the Prairie Region, generally (for example, as measured by seasonal employment as a
    percentage of total employment), the problem is nonetheless significantly greater here than
    it is in central Canada and in the country as a whole. See Richard Beaudry, Le chomage
    saisonnier et l'explication des disparites interrigimales de chomage air Canada, Discussion
    Paper no. 84 (Ottawa: Economic Council of Canada, 1977).

2. For example, the successful drive toward agricultural self-sufficiency in many undeveloped
    or less-developed nations (such as China and India), combined with government
    commitments in many developed countries to protect their agricultural sectors via
    subsidization and import restrictions, represent serious threats to the Western Canadian
    grain industry.

3. It might be noted that, with conventional techniques, only about one-third of the oil in a
    reservoir can be recovered; even with existing enhanced-recovery technology, this recovery
    rate can be increased substantially. Many enhanced oil-recovery, heavy-oil, and oil-sands
    projects in the province are economically viable even when oil prices are as low as $25 (U.S.)
    per barrel.

4. See R.W. Wright and R.L. Mansell, "An Evaluation of Gas Protection Alternatives for
    Alberta in a Market-Oriented Pricing Environment" (Study submitted by Pan-Alberta Gas
    Limited to the Energy Resources Conservation Board hearings on Gas Surplus
    Determination, December 1986).

gas resources largely uneconomical and would, cause the resources themselves to become redundant, constitutes a greater threat than physical exhaustion of the province's conventional reserves.

The Relevant Economic Variables

A significant shortcoming in the literature on regional economic instability is the lack of attention paid to the issue of the variable or variables that should be used in measuring instability. While the variables typically used include one, or a combination, of output, income, employment, and the unemployment rate, no attempts are made to base the selection on an economically meaningful link between instability and the costs of instability. Although changes in many of these variables are often highly correlated, the fact remains that the "costs" associated with variations in, say, regional output would generally differ from those associated with swings in, say, per-capita income or employment. Much the same distinction can be made between predictable (foreseeable) and unpredictable (unforeseeable) swings in a particular variable. Such differentiations are also important from a policy viewpoint, because a particular stabilization policy could well lead to less variability in one variable but more in another.

It is not possible, within the confines of this study, to develop a comprehensive and consistent theoretical framework to address this issue. Instead, we shall present measures of instability for a cross-section of variables, which are listed below, along with some brief comments on their implications for economic costs.

1. Regional Gross Domestic Product (GDP), or value added, is a measure of output produced within the geographical boundaries of the region. As such, it is an indicator of economic activity within the region; it is not, however, especially for Alberta, an accurate indicator of incomes received by residents of the region. For example, a significant proportion of Alberta's GDP is in the form of resource rents collected by governments or otherwise distributed to lenders and owners outside Alberta.[5] Thus, while a high degree of variability in provincial GDP may well have serious implications for the instability of government revenues or corporate profits, it does not necessarily translate into equivalent instability in personal incomes or employment.

2. Personal income is defined as wages, salaries and supplemental labor income; military pay and allowances; net income of farm operators and unincorporated businesses; interest; dividend and miscellaneous investment

---

5. For example, in 1985, personal income received by Albertans represented slightly more than 60 percent of the province's GDP (Alberta Bureau of Statistics, Alberta Economic Accounts, 1985 [Edmonton: Alberta Treasury, 1986], tables 2 and 7).

income; and transfer payments from governments, corporations, and nonresidents. Thus, regional personal income is a measure of income received by the residents of the region. For Alberta, instability in this variable would generally be expected to have more serious and immediate consequences for the economic welfare of the province's population than would equivalent variability in GDP.

3. Per-capita personal income is typically used as a measure of the average welfare of a region's population. It is a function of income per worker, the labor-force participation rate, the unemployment rate, and the age structure of the population.[6] Hence, variations in per-capita income embody variations in these constituent elements. In general, instability in this measure is a more serious concern than is an equivalent degree of instability in total personal income. This is because of the important role played by interregional migration, especially in the case of Alberta. As outlined earlier (see Chapter 3), changes in total income bring about significant changes in the provincial population (via migration), which substantially reduce variations in per-capita income. This is not to suggest, however, that such adjustments are costless. Indeed, along with the economic and social costs associated with migration, there are substantial costs associated with variations in population growth rates, particularly when they are unpredictable.[7]

4. Employment is perhaps the single most important variable from a policy perspective, because it is a primary determinant of economic welfare and, in our work-oriented value system, of social status. In addition, the jobs gained or lost in a region, along with the rate of unemployment, tend to be the most visible and widely publicized measures of economic health. The social and economic costs associated with instability in regional employment are therefore generally viewed as particularly significant, despite the cost-reducing or cost-averaging effects of programs such as unemployment insurance and welfare.

Regardless of the variable or variables used to assess regional economic instability, it is important to distinguish between expected and unexpected variations. For example, to the extent that cycles in average incomes are predictable, it may be possible for households to reduce the costs of

6. Specifically, Personal income per capita (Yp/P) can be expressed as

$(Yp/P) = [Yp/N][(p)(P1/P)(1-u)]$

where P = population, N = number employed, p = labor-force participation rate, $P1$ = noninstitutionalized population 15 years and over, and u = unemployment rate.

7. For example, an unexpected or unplanned increase leads to a strain on the social infrastructure; conversely, an unexpected decrease results in excess infrastructure capacity and associated costs in the form of higher per-capita taxes, loss of homeowners' equity, etc.

instability through higher saving rates or other types of stabilizing behavior such as cyclical changes in household labor-force participation or changes in household debt patterns. The costs associated with unexpected variations, on the other hand, would generally be larger, since *ex ante* adjustments are ruled out. Thus, in many cases, the consequences or costs of instability will depend on the extent to which variations are anticipated.

Also relevant here is the distinction between systematic and unsystematic risk.[8] In a regional context, unpredictable variations in a specific industry or sector would constitute unsystematic risk. An example might be a technological breakthrough in the transmission of electricity that substantially reduces the markets for Alberta's natural gas. Clearly, unsystematic risk can be reduced or eliminated by expanding the region's portfolio of basic industries – that is, through industrial diversification. In contrast, systematic risk would be associated with the kind of unanticipated swings in economic activity, policy, or trade patterns, that would affect *most* industries or sectors (albeit to different degrees). Industrial diversification might reduce this type of risk somewhat, but it cannot eliminate it.

In order to apply these concepts to an analysis of regional economic instability, it would ideally be necessary to answer three fundamental questions:

1. Which variations are systematic and, hence, in a theoretical sense, predictable, and which are random?

2. Given the level of sophistication of the economic agents (firms and households) in the regional economy, which of the systematic variations would generally be anticipated? In other words, how are expectations formed?

3. For which of the expected systematic variations are there viable behavioral adjustments that can be made by these agents to reduce the costs associated with instability?

Unfortunately, there are no easy or definitive answers to these questions, which are both complex and largely unexplored in the literature. We can offer only the following rather general observations:

1. The fluctuations in energy policy, prices,and markets and in agricultural prices and production that have created so much instability in the Alberta economy are more likely of the random (unpredictable) variety than of the cyclical (predictable) variety. If there is a general theory that could predict these fluctuations, it is certainly not well known or commonly used.

---

8. The concepts of systematic and unsystematic risk are widely used in financial theory, particularly in the context of capital-asset pricing.

2. With the exception of short-term trends that follow a major shock, individuals, firms, and governments do not seem to have a very good track record in predicting major swings in the Alberta economy or in identifying the causal factors. For example, the widespread bankruptcies, foreclosures, and overcapacity that have occurred in many sectors would suggest that the adversities experienced since 1981 were mostly unforeseen.

3. This experience would also indicate that expectations tend to be more extrapolative or adaptive than rational.[9] Indeed, the fact that energy policies, energy investment plans, and institutional lending patterns during the late 1970s and early 1980s were based on projections of continued rapid escalation in energy prices suggests that, even for "sophisticated" agents, extrapolative expectations dominate. The prospects for finding rational-expectations formation in consumer behavior may be brighter.

4. For a variety of practical reasons, the opportunities for individual agents to adopt stabilizing behavior, even when economic swings are foreseen, may be quite limited. That is, although savings rates and debt-equity ratios, for example, can be adjusted, their stabilizing effects will often be overwhelmed by changes in the macro economy. Consider the case of a downturn in the provincial economy that manifests itself in reduced incomes, less employment, and substantial outmigration. In this situation, many firms that rely on local markets will be swept away by the tide of falling demand, and, in such an environment, the difference between a well-run firm prepared for market instability and an average firm that is unprepared will likely prove insignificant. Similarly, a household directly affected by the layoffs and rapidly falling housing prices will find its economic survival threatened very quickly. Even with above-average savings accumulated in the expectation of instability, a typical household would have only a very limited ability to weather a downturn even of relatively short duration. Furthermore, with falling or perhaps even negative equity in housing, it would be difficult to borrow funds in order to bridge such a downturn.[10]

On the basis of these observations, it seems reasonable, as a first approximation, to focus on total instability rather than on the distinction between foreseeable, foreseen, and compensated variations, on the one hand, and unforeseeable variations, on the other. We shall make only a very limited attempt at such a distinction, using the concept of permanent income.

---

9. Simply stated, the notion of "rational expectations" is based on the promise that people do not systematically ignore readily available information that could be used to improve their decisions. Extrapolative expectations are those that extrapolate from recent trends, while adaptive expectations incorporate adjustments based on previous forecast errors.

10. As mentioned earlier, equity in housing represents the bulk of the average family's assets. It is often the only collateral for a loan that most lending institutions will accept.

Indexes of Regional Economic Instability

Many alternative statistical measures of regional economic instability (REI) can be found in the literature. For example, M. E. Conroy and John E. Kort use the standard deviation from its trend value of variable X (for example, regional income or employment), relative to either the mean value of X or its trend value. In contrast, the Economic Council of Canada uses the average absolute and percentage deviations from the trend value.[11] In short, there is neither a perfect measure of instability nor a consensus as to which measure is best overall.

There are three main differences among the various measures commonly used. The first involves the weighting of the deviations.[12] The indices that employ squared deviations are more sensitive measures of instability than are those that use absolute deviations. But, in some cases, the advantages of this greater sensitivity may be offset by unrealistic underlying assumptions regarding the "costs" of variability. For example, with squared deviations, the implicit assumption is that a single deviation of two percent is twice as serious as two deviations of one percent. The second main difference lies in the method employed to arrive at the benchmark for calculating deviations. The main alternatives are (1) some moving average of historical values or (2) values based on a linear, quadratic, or exponential trend line. Associated with these variations are important differences in the underlying assumptions regarding the manner in which expectations are formed.[13] The third difference is that some indices of instability can be "decomposed,"

---

11. M. E. Conroy, "The Concept and Measurement of Regional Industrial Diversification," Southern Economic Journal 41 (1975): 492-505; John R. Kort, "Regional Economic Instability and Industrial Diversification in the U.S.," Land Economics 57 (1981): 596-608; Economic Council of Canada, Western Transition.

12. For variable X, the unweighted coefficient of variation is defined as

$$\left[\frac{\sum_{t} (X_t - \bar{X})^2}{N - 1} \right]^{1/2} \div X$$

where $\bar{X}$ is the mean and X_t.

Other measures of instability are discussed in O. Knudsen and A. Parnes, Trade Instability and Economic Growth (Toronto: Lexington Books, 1975), and P. A. Yotopoulos and J. B. Nugent, Economics of Development: Empirical Investigations (New York: Harper and Row, 1976).

13. For example, in the moving-average approach, the implicit assumption is that expectations at time t are based only on a limited number of observations preceding t. Where a (fitted) trend line is used, on the other hand, the underlying assumption is that expectations are based on all observations made during the sample period.

while others cannot. Since an important objective of this chapter is to isolate the sources of instability, as well as to measure the degree of instability, this is a key criterion for choosing among the alternatives.

The primary REI index selected for our analysis is as follows:

$$(4.1) \quad REI = \left[\frac{\sum\limits_{t} (X_t - \hat{X}_t)^2}{(N-3)\bar{X}^2} \right]^{1/2}$$

X_t is the actual value of the regional variable under consideration (eg. income or employment) in year t; $\bar{X}$ is the mean value; N is the number of observations; and $\hat{X}_t$ is the trend value. The latter is defined by:

$$\hat{X}_t = \hat{B}_0 + \hat{B}_1(t) + \hat{B}_2(t^2),$$

where $\hat{B}_0$, $\hat{B}_1$ and $\hat{B}_2$ are least-squares estimates.

As shown by Postner and Wesa (1985), this index can be disaggregated or decomposed.[14] For example, suppose X_t is total employment in the region and it is made up of X_{1t}, employment in sector 1, and X_{2t} employment in sector 2. For this case, it can be shown that the index of REI set out in (4.1) above can be decomposed as follows:

$$(4.2) \quad REI = a^2 \frac{\sum\limits_{t} (X_{1t} - \hat{X}_{1t})^2}{(N-3)\bar{X}_1^2} + b^2 \frac{\sum\limits_{t} (X_{2t} - \hat{X}_{2t})^2}{(N-3)\bar{X}_2^2}$$

$$+ 2ab \frac{\sum\limits_{t} (X_{1t} - \hat{X}_{1t})(X_{2t} - \hat{X}_{2t})}{(N-3)\bar{X}_1 \bar{X}_2}$$

where $a = \bar{X}_1/\bar{X}$, $b = \bar{X}_2/\bar{X}$ and $\hat{X}_{1t}$ and $\hat{X}_{2t}$ are estimated in the same way as $\hat{X}_t$. In other words, total instability equals the weighted sum of the variance of sector 1 employment, the variance of sector 2 employment, and the covariance of sector 1 and sector 2 employment.[15] The weights are based on

---

14. Harry H. Postner and Lesle M. Wesa, Employment Instability in Western Canada: A Diversification Analysis of the Manufacturing and Other Sectors, Discussion Paper no. 275 (Ottawa: Economic Council of Canada, 1985).

15. Using matrix notation,

$$REI = [a \ b] \begin{bmatrix} X_1^* X_1 & X_1^* X_2 \\ X_2^* X_1 & X_2^* X_2 \end{bmatrix} \begin{bmatrix} a \\ b \end{bmatrix}$$

where $X_1^* X_1$ and $X_2^* X_2$ are, respectively, the variances of X_1 and X_2, and $X_1^* X_2$ (or $X_2^* X_1$) is the covariance between X_1 and X_2.

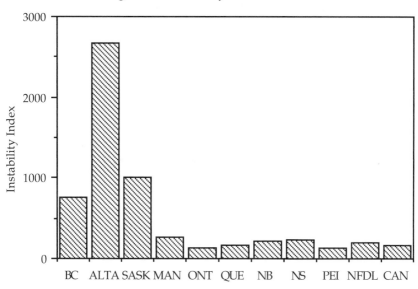

Figure 22. Variability of GDP, 1961-1985

Value of Index for Yukon and NWT is 4667

Index is

$$\text{REI (index of regional economic instability)} = \left[\frac{\sum\limits_{t} (X_t - \hat{X}_t)^2}{(N - 3)\bar{X}^2} \right]^{1/2}$$

where X = actual value of variable, $\hat{X}$ = trend value of X, $\bar{X}$ = mean value of X; N = no. of observations.

Data Source: Statistics Canada (61-510 and Cansim D20031).

the industry shares of total employment. Furthermore, this decomposition is easily generalized to any number of components, although there is a rapid escalation in the number of terms since all pairwise covariances must be taken into account.

Alberta's Relative Instability: Some Provincial Comparisons

Using data from the Provincial Economic Accounts[16] for the 1961-85 period, values for the REI index were computed for GDP, personal income and per-capita personal income. These are presented in Table 4 and depicted in Figures 22 and 23. It is important to note that the values shown represent an

---

16. These accounts are published by Statistics Canada, Cat. no. 13-201.

Figure 23. Variability of Total and Per Capita Personal Income, 1961-1985

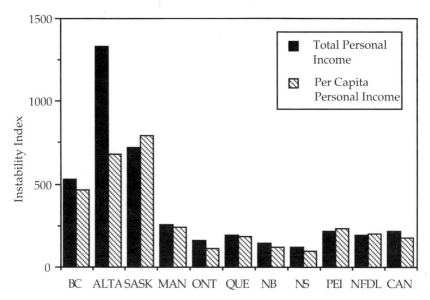

Value of Yukon and NWT for total personal income is 336 and for per capita income is 329.

Data Source: Statistics Canada (13-201).

ordinal rather than a cardinal measure of instability; for example, the value of the personal income, REI index is 1,328 for Alberta compared with 159 for Ontario. Thus, although it can be concluded that personal income shows much greater variability in Alberta than it does in Ontario, it does not follow that Alberta's instability problem, in terms of personal income, is 1,328/159, or 8.4 times the size that of Ontario's. As noted earlier, the REI index employs squared deviations and hence attaches proportionally greater weight to larger deviations than to smaller ones.

In any case, it is clear from these results that the Alberta economy tends to be one of the most unstable regional economies in Canada. In terms of variability of GDP, it ranks second only to the economy of the Yukon and Northwest Territories, and, with respect to personal income, it is the most unstable of all regional economies. The degree of variability in per-capita income is somewhat smaller, no doubt as a result of the smoothing effects of transfers and interregional migration. Even here, however, the degree of instability is only exceeded by that of Saskatchewan.[17] Furthermore,

---

17. It is interesting to note that the rankings shown in Figure 23 for per-capita-income instability correspond to those obtained by the Economic Council of Canada using a different index and a sample period ending in 1981 (Western Transition, table 2-3).

Table 4. Indices of Gross Domestic Product and Income Instability for Canada's Provinces[a]

Gross Domestic Product Instability	
Prince Edward Island	139
Ontario	140
Quebec	159
Canada	*169*
Newfoundland	200
New Brunswick	220
Nova Scotia	224
Manitoba	268
British Columbia	751
Saskatchewan	1,000
Alberta	2,672
Yukon and Northwest Territories	4,667
Personal Income Instability	
Nova Scotia	124
New Brunswick	141
Ontario	159
Quebec	194
Newfoundland	194
Prince Edward Island	215
Canada	*216*
Manitoba	254
Yukon and Northwet Territories	336
British Columbia	533
Saskatchewan	720
Alberta	1,328
Per Capita Personal Income Instability	
Nova Scotia	100
Ontario	115
New Brunswick	122
Canada	*176*
Quebec	181
Newfoundland	201
Prince Edward Island	235
Manitoba	237
Yukon and Northwet Territories	329
British Columbia	463
Alberta	685
Saskatchewan	793

[a] Based on data for the 1961-85 period.

Source: Based on data from Statistics Canada, *Provincial Economic Accounts*, 1961-85.

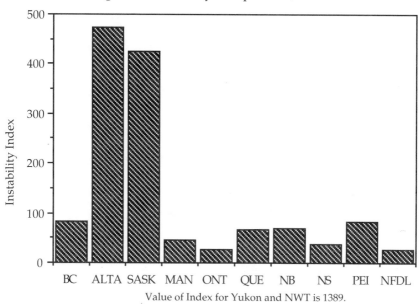

Figure 24. Variability of Population, 1961-1985

Value of Index for Yukon and NWT is 1389.

Data Source: Statistics Canada (91-210).

Alberta's instability in terms of all three measures is much greater than the national average and substantially greater than that for the most stable provincial economies.

We shall present a detailed analysis of employment instability in the next section of this chapter. Here it will suffice to note that the regional pattern for this variable parallels the pattern for personal income. The REI index for employment, for example, using the same sample period, is 183 for Alberta, compared with 34 for Canada and 30 for Ontario. This correspondence should not be surprising, since employment income typically accounts for over 70 percent of personal income.[18]

Much the same picture emerges from an examination of population instability. As shown in Figure 24 (and Table 5), Alberta's REI index value for population (once again using the 1961-85 period) is large in comparison with that of all regions except Saskatchewan and the Northwest Territories. Much of this instability can be explained by the dominant role of migration in regional population-growth-rate variations,[19] combined with the

---

18. In 1984, for example, for Canada, the sum of wages, salaries, supplemental labor income, military pay and allowances, and net income from unincorporated businesses amounted to 72 percent of total Personal Income.

19. See Marc G. Termote, "The Growth and Redistribution of the Canadian Population," in Still Living Together, ed. Coffey and Polese, table 2.

Table 5. Index of Population Instability for Canada's Provinces[a]

Population Instability	
Ontario	26
Newfoundland	27
Nova Scotia	38
Manitoba	46
Quebec	67
New Brunswick	69
Prince Edward Island	83
British Columbia	84
Saskatchewan	426
Alberta	473
Yukon and Northwest Territories	1,389

[a]Based on data from the 1961-85 period.

Data Source: Statistics Canadda, *Vital Statistics*, Cat. no.8-201, varios issues.

sensitivity of interregional migration to changes in relative regional income and employment conditions.

Employment is a particularly important indicator of social well-being because of the income it produces and because of its significance as a source of acceptance and self-esteem in our work-oriented society. The costs associated with employment instability are therefore visible, direct, and substantial. In this regard, Alberta once again scores poorly. In fact, it exhibits the greatest employment variability in Canada and, as illustrated in Figure 25, to a degree considerably higher than both the national average and that in Texas and Oklahoma, the two U.S. states whose economic base is similar to Alberta's. The latter difference is particularly noticeable when the degrees of instability of the U.S. and Canadian regions are compared to their respective national averages.

The unavoidable conclusion is that Alberta's economic instability is indeed a very serious problem. Regardless of the variable used, the province tends to exhibit much greater variability than does the country as a whole and, indeed, than does any other province. Moreover, it is evident that, although the 1982-85 experience accounts for a substantial portion of the unusually large measures of instability, the problem is not limited to this period.

One drawback of these indices is that the selection of the measure of instability is rather arbitrary. In particular, the selection of the functional form to determine the expected component of the index – "the trend" – implicitly incorporates rather strong assumptions regarding expectations formation, without making explicit the underlying behavioral assumptions.

Figure 25. Variability of Employment in Selected Regions, 1961-1985

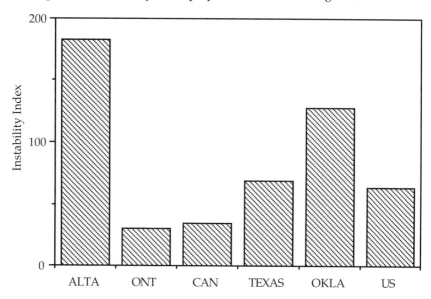

Data Source: Statistics Canada (71-201) and U.S. Department of Commerce, Employment and Earnings, States and Areas.

It is possible, however, to construct indices of instability that are more firmly rooted in economic theory. The drawback here is that these competing approaches require considerable data and often involve relatively sophisticated statistical analysis. The results of assessments of the Alberta economy's instability in the context of a model of transitory and permanent income flows confirm that the degree of instability in Alberta is high relative to that in the rest of Canada.

As an alternative to the assumption of expected income as a linear trend, it was assumed that the observed time series of the variable in question was the realization of a stochastic process, and that the anticipated or expected component could be modeled using an autoregressive integrated moving average (ARIMA) representation. This model is consistent with the notion that economic agents have knowledge of the underlying economic process generating the time series and utilize it efficiently to form expectations about its future levels. Time-series properties of real personal per-capita and real disposable per-capita incomes for the period 1950-84 for Alberta, Ontario, and Canada were investigated, and it was found that the stochastic process underlying the data in all three cases could be derived by first differencing the data. Those transformed data yielded a model of the underlying stochastic process from which estimates of anticipated and unanticipated

income could be derived. The residuals of the model constitute the
unanticipated or transitory component of income, while the equation
describing the stochastic process yields predictions of anticipated values. The
index of instability, I, is defined as the sum of squares of unanticipated
income (**UI**), normalized by anticipated income (**PI**).

$$(4.3) \quad I = \left[\sum_t \left[\frac{UI}{PI} \right] \right]^{1/2} \cdot \frac{1}{N}$$

where I is the index of instability for the measure of income in question, and
n is the sample size. The numerator is an estimate of the variance of
unanticipated income. The index is thus the normalized variance of the
unanticipated component of income.

The results in Table 6 are interesting in two respects. First, they confirm
the notion that income instability in Alberta is much greater than it is in
Ontario and Canada. Second, the differences between the instability indices
of personal and disposable income shed light on government tax policy and
its effects on levels of instability. For Ontario and Canada, the index of
instability of transitory income based on real disposable income exceeds the
corresponding index for real personal income, while the reverse holds true
for Alberta. The basic difference between personal income and disposable
income is taxes. That the index of instability of real personal per-capita
income exceeds that of real disposable per-capita income in Alberta suggests
that tax policy in the province has tended to lessen the degree of instability.
This result offers support for the claim by Carmichael that, in Alberta, the
provincial government has implemented countercyclical fiscal policies at
least with respect to taxes, whereas in most of the other provinces,
governments have been forced to implement procyclical policies because of
the constraints of government deficits.[20]

It is also possible to use this model of anticipated and unanticipated
income to assess the consequences of instability for aggregate economic
variables and to ascertain differences between provinces in their response to
instability. The approach involves taking the time-series estimates of
unanticipated income and statistically analyzing their influence on time
series of important variables such as investment (proxied by building
permits), unemployment, and net migration for the period 1950 to 1984.

The results of this exercise for Alberta and Ontario are revealing in that
they highlight differences in the adjustment of the two provincial economies
to unanticipated economic shocks. The unemployment rate in Alberta and

20. Carmichael, New Stresses on Confederation, p. 19.

Table 6. Indices of Instability for Per Capita
Personal and Disposal Income, 1950-84

	Real Personal Per Capita Income	Real Disposal Per Capita Income
Alberta	.072	.0695
Ontario	.0129	.0170
Canada	.0180	.0196

Source: Based on data from Statistics Canada, *Provincial Economic Accounts*, Cat. no. 13-213.

Ontario was found to be inversely related to movements in the current value of unanticipated real personal income per capita, with unemployment in Ontario being more responsive. In the case of net migration, the rate for Ontario was found to be unresponsive to movements in real personal and disposable income for either lagged or current values. For Alberta, net migration was positively related to movements in current values of unanticipated real disposable income per capita. Investment, as measured by the value of building permits, was found to be highly responsive in both provinces to current period movements in unanticipated real personal and disposable income per capita. The responsiveness (in terms of elasticities evaluated at the mean) of the value of building permits in Alberta to movements in unanticipated income consistently exceeded that of Ontario.

The evidence thus suggests that Alberta has a dual problem with respect to instability. Not only is its level of instability higher than that of Ontario, but the responsiveness of its key economic aggregates to unanticipated shocks is also greater. While variations in unemployment rates are a mechanism of adjustment common to both provinces, the Alberta economy also relies upon net interprovincial migration. Both provincial economies experience variability in investment levels in response to unanticipated movements in income, but the responsiveness of Alberta exceeds that of Ontario.

Sources of Instability

In an attempt to identify the factors underlying Alberta's unusually high degree of economic instability, we decomposed a number of the REI indices outlined above. The most revealing results were obtained from the sectoral decomposition of the index of employment instability (as summarized in Table 7). It should be noted that the caveats we raised in relation to the overall indices apply here as well. Recall, in particular, that the deviations are squared and, therefore, a variance of, say, 100 for agriculture, compared with, say, 50 for manufacturing does not mean that employment in agriculture is twice as variable as employment in manufacturing. To keep the comparisons manageable, we have presented results only for Alberta, Ontario, and Canada.

As indicated by the diagonal elements in the matrices in Table 7, employment in all Alberta sector's but one shows considerably greater variability than it does in the corresponding sectors of the Ontario and Canadian economies. The exception is the mining (MIN) sector, which has a variance of 1,268, compared with Ontario's 1,712. But, as shown by the distribution of employment in the first column, this sector accounts for less than one percent of Ontario's employment (as an average over the 1961-85 period), while it represents 5.4 percent in the case of Alberta. As such, this variability, despite being smaller than Ontario's has a much greater significance for Alberta.

It can also be observed that, compared with the situation in Ontario and Canada as a whole, Alberta has a higher concentration of employment in agriculture (AGR), mining (MIN), and construction (CON) and that in each of these sectors in Alberta, the variability is particularly large. For example, in agriculture, it is 1,123 in Alberta compared with 392 in Ontario; in construction, 1,412 in Alberta compared with 205 in Ontario. Only in the case of trade (TRA) is the degree of employment variability comparable in the two regions.

The values for the covariance terms (the off-diagonal terms in Table 7) are even more revealing. Recall that negative covariance between sectors (that is, where employment tends to fluctuate in opposite directions in the two sectors) serves to reduce overall variability, while positive covariance serves to increase it. In this regard, two important differences are evident from comparisons between Alberta and Ontario. First, there are many instances of negative covariance in Ontario – every one of the province's sectors shows negative covariance with at least one other sector – whereas in Alberta, only in agriculture does employment vary in a direction opposite to that in other sectors. In other words, agriculture is the only countercyclical sector in Alberta. Second, in comparison with Ontario, the covariance among industries in Alberta tends to be much greater in magnitude than it is in Ontario.

A definitive analysis of the causes of Alberta's instability problem is beyond the scope of this study, but some of the more obvious factors can be usefully noted. First, as explained in Chapter 2, energy policies have been particularly destabilizing to Alberta's key oil and gas sector, especially in

Table 7. Sectoral Disaggregation of the Regional Economic Instability Index for Employment in Alberta, Ontario, and Canada, 1961-85

%EMP		AGR	MIN	MAN	CON	TCU	TRA	FIN	SER	GOV
					Alberta					
9.34	AGR	1,123	-711	-177	-555	-253	-112	-558	-69	-43
5.41	MIN	-711	1,268	632	971	442	169	469	160	145
8.92	MAN	-177	632	741	690	235	215	370	97	283
8.77	CON	-555	971	690	1,412	323	250	673	144	359
8.64	TCU	-253	442	235	323	219	75	167	58	33
18.10	TRA	-112	169	215	250	75	93	151	30	85
5.20	FIN	-558	469	370	673	187	151	576	84	240
28.50	SER	-69	160	97	144	58	30	84	46	74
7.12	GOV	-43	145	283	359	33	85	240	74	303
					Ontario					
3.37	AGR	392	-102	191	-92	98	-14	-38	2	-120
0.96	MIN	-102	1,712	115	95	106	-87	7	55	221
24.91	MAN	191	115	195	33	101	26	21	-13	-36
5.64	CON	-92	95	33	205	36	99	36	2	58
7.26	TCU	98	106	101	36	77	18	-2	-11	-8
16.76	TRA	-14	-87	26	99	18	80	11	10	15
5.97	FIN	-38	7	21	36	-2	11	69	-20	6
28.36	SER	2	55	-13	-2	-11	10	-20	27	11
6.78	GOV	-120	-221	-36	58	-8	15	6	11	71
					Canada					
4.96	AGR	37	92	56	21	35	25	3	18	-3
1.62	MIN	92	649	269	119	127	98	82	76	24
20.17	MAN	56	269	203	55	84	51	32	32	-34
5.98	CON	21	119	55	105	25	45	7	7	11
8.40	TCU	35	127	84	25	55	30	4	21	-15
17.36	TRA	25	98	51	45	30	33	14	11	1
5.39	FIN	3	82	32	7	4	14	45	1	9
29.09	SER	18	76	32	7	21	11	1	16	3
7.04	GOV	-3	24	-34	11	-15	1	9	3	31

Source: Based on data from Statistics Canada, Cat. no.71-001. AGR = Agriculture; MIN = Mining; MAN = Manufacturing; CON = Construction; TCU = Transportation, Communication and Utilities; TRA = Trade; FIN = Finance, Insurance and Real Estate; SER = Services; GOV = Government.

combination with the large fluctuations in international energy prices that
have occurred since the early 1970s. Second, Alberta's agricultural sector is
largely unprotected from the vagaries of the international marketplace. For
example, in comparison with the situation in Ontario, agricultural activities
in Alberta tend to be **less** concentrated in the areas that afford a higher
degree of stability – that is, in areas such as dairies, and, poultry, which have
adopted supply-management systems and/or focus on local markets or
processing. In other words, its greater concentration on livestock and grain
production for export no doubt explains, to a significant extent, of the high
degree of variability in Alberta's agricultural sector.

A third factor contributing to Alberta's instability is the high degree of
capital intensity in the province's primary sectors, combined with the fact
that investment, especially by the oil and gas sector, is a key driving force in
many of its secondary and service industries. Not only is investment
generally the least stable component of aggregate demand, but there is an
added element of variability in energy investment because of the
unpredictable nature of energy prices and policies. Furthermore, this
variability is transmitted to the provincial economy through swings in
energy rents. Because rent tax or royalty revenue constitutes a large
proportion of the provincial government's total revenue, these fluctuations
tend to cause variations in government expenditures, and hence in the many
sectors driven by those expenditures.

Finally, the Alberta economy is much more dependent on both primary
production and foreign markets than are, say, the Quebec and Ontario
economies.[21] International markets, especially for primary products, are
subject to large swings, and, for Alberta's basic industries, there is no
equivalent to the Auto Pact to provide stability through market integration
and preferential market access. The resulting variability has been further
compounded, at least in the period since the late 1960s, by federal tax and
expenditure policies that, taken as a whole, have acted to deflate the Alberta
economy during both its upturns and its downturns.

Future Directions of the Alberta Economy

Before we examine the various policies that might be pursued to achieve
greater economic stability, it might be useful to comment briefly on the
general directions in which the Alberta economy is headed and the areas of
vulnerability and potential adversity likely to be encountered along the way.

---

21. For data on interprovincial and international trade by region, see H. M. Pinchin, The
     Regional Impact of the Canadian Tariff (Ottawa: Economic Council of Canada, 1979).

Here, the main objective is to assess the degree to which the forces of instability that have been evident in the past are likely to remain active in the future and,on that basis, to consider the relative importance of existing policies aimed at stabilizing the Alberta economy.

Since the first quarter of 1987, the Alberta economy has shown signs of steady, albeit modest, recovery.[22] In general, this would appear to be attributable to six main factors: the improved health of the energy sector and the associated increases in energy investment; the strength of the livestock component of the agricultural sector, combined with substantial federal and provincial agricultural assistance; the "trickle-down" effects of strong economic growth in the United States and central Canada; the improved expectations and credit conditions with respect to investment generally; the stimulative posture of provincial fiscal policy; and the economy's fundamental strengths as outlined in Chapter 3 (adaptability of the labor force, flexibility of input costs, etc.), which continue to translate into high rates of new business formation and employment creation, especially in the services sector.

Although the prospects for the continuation of these trends into the near future generally appear to be favorable, they are in fact very uncertain. On the positive side, one can point to the recent improvements in grain prices, the high and rising levels of oil and gas production (which, in the case of gas, can be largely attributed to market and price deregulation in Canada and the United States), the strong recovery of petrochemical prices, the expected continued growth of the Canadian and U.S. economies (at least to mid-1990), and the improved fiscal position of the provincial government. In addition, the Free Trade Agreement with the United States, is expected to have particularly favorable implications for the Alberta economy,[23] especially for its petrochemical, cattle, hog, and lumber industries.

Unfortunately, there are at least as many factors within the bounds of reasonable expectation that could cut this recovery short and reestablish the tendencies toward instability. Such factors include the following: drought

22. For example, from the first quarter of 1987 to the first quarter of 1988, the seasonally adjusted unemployment rate in Alberta has fallen from 10.3 percent to 8.2 percent, and migration has moved from a net outflow of 1,820 people in the first quarter of 1987 to a net inflow of 120 people in the first quarter of 1988 (based on data from the Alberta Bureau of Statistics, Alberta Statistical Review, First Quarter 1988 [May 1988], tables 4 and 13).

23. For a convenient summary of the sectoral and overall impacts of free trade on the Alberta economy, see Katie Macmillan, Putting the Cards on the Table: Free Trade and Western Canadian Industries (Calgary: Canada West Foundation, 1986). See also "The Conference on Free Trade" (Unpublished proceedings of a conference held at the Palliser Hotel, Calgary, November 12, 1987).

conditions in the province, combined with a voter backlash against continued high levels of agricultural assistance and subsidization; continued weakness and variability of oil and gas prices, along with the curtailment of the CEDIP program and the phasing-out of the provincial royalty holiday and royalty tax-credit programs;[24] further increases in interest rates and appreciation of the Canadian dollar (vis-a-vis the U.S. dollar), both of which can be expected to have particularly unfavorable impacts on the province's basic economic sectors;[25] and a rebounding of the provincial deficit (because of declining energy prices and royalties), combined with the resulting reductions in provincial government expenditures. In addition, there remain, especially over the longer run, considerable "policy threats" to the full recovery of the Alberta economy. It is interesting, for example that the Free Trade Agreement is frequently criticized for precluding, or at least making more difficult, reintroduction of a National Energy Program. One can only conclude from this that such a program remains popular in the politically powerful regions of the country and may well be reintroduced if (or when) energy prices rise significantly. Any program comparable to the NEP can be expected to throw the Alberta economy into recession and create another round of instability.

It is clear from these considerations that the continued recovery and increased future stability of the Alberta economy are far from certain. In fact, most of the sources of extreme variability in the past still remain, and, in the absence of new policies, there is no reason to expect that variability will cease to be a serious problem. The various responses that might improve this situation are taken up in Chapter 5.

24. Previously, there was considerable scope for cost reductions to offset the effects of reduced prices, but it will now be difficult to achieve any further significant downward adjustments in these costs. Thus, additional declines in prices, increases in net royalties and taxes, appreciation of the Canadian dollar, and increases in interest rates can be expected to result in significant reductions in oil and gas investment.

25. This is so because these sectors tend to be very capital intensive (and, hence, highly sensitive to changes in the cost of financial capital), and because the prices of their output tend to be set in terms of U.S. dollars (so that an appreciation of the Canadian dollar results in a one-for-one decrease in the Canadian dollar prices).

Summary

It is apparent from the results summarized in this section that, based on data for the 1961-85 period, and in terms of most measures, Alberta has the most variable regional economy in Canada. The level of instability in the province's GDP exceeds that of every region, except the Yukon and Northwest Territories. In total personal income, population, and employment, Alberta exhibits significantly greater instability than does any other province (only Saskatchewan comes close to rivalling Alberta for this dubious distinction). And although the variability in per-capita income is somewhat less extreme, it nonetheless exceeds, by a wide margin, that of every other province except Saskatchewan and British Columbia. Furthermore, the degree of employment instability is not only considerably greater in Alberta than in the other provinces, but it also far exceeds that of U.S. states such as Oklahoma and Texas, which have economic bases similar to Alberta's. Although the large swing in the province's economic performance in the 1980-85 period contributes significantly to the large values of its instability indices, it is clear from the analysis (which is based on data dating back to 1961) that Alberta's instability problem existed long before this most recent experience.

In an attempt to isolate the main sources of this problem, we undertook a sectoral decomposition of the instability indices and compared the results for Alberta with those for Ontario, the benchmark province, as well as with those for the nation as a whole. Three main conclusions emerged from this analysis:

1. Alberta's basic (primary) sectors are especially variable both in absolute terms and relative to their counterparts in other regions:

2   most of the other sectors in the province (in particular, construction; manufacturing; transportation, communication, and utilities; and finance, insurance, and real estate) are also much more variable than are their counterparts in Ontario, and this variability appears to be closely linked to fluctuations in Alberta's energy sector;

3   unlike the situation in Ontario, Alberta's industries exhibited few instances of negative covariance, and this serves to amplify the province's overall economic instability.

Some of these patterns can be explained by the factors that contributed to the downturn of the Alberta economy in the early 1980s. Of particular importance here are the energy policies, combined with the fluctuations in international energy prices, that were very destabilizing for the province's oil and gas industry, and hence for the overall provincial economy. Other factors include the greater exposure of Alberta's agricultural sector (compared with Ontario's) to the vagaries of the international marketplace; the high capital intensity of the province's primary sectors, combined with the fact that investment, especially in the oil and gas sector, is particularly unstable, and that this investment is a key driving force for many of Alberta's secondary and service sectors; the greater dependence of the Alberta economy (compared with that of Ontario) on primary production and international markets both of which tend to exhibit considerable variability; and the compounding effects, at least since the late 1960s, of federal tax and expenditure policies, which, taken together, have worked to deflate the Alberta economy.

Finally, we have concluded that most of the sources of extreme variability in the past still exist today, and, in the absence of effective policies, economic instability can be expected to remain a serious problem in Alberta in the foreseeable future.

5 Dealing with Economic Instability

The preceding chapters have shown that the Alberta economy exhibits a degree of cyclical and random instability that is inordinately high by both regional and national standards. Whether they are measured in social or purely economic terms, the costs of this extreme variability are unquestionably large. They include the considerable (and avoidable) dislocations that affect families, businesses, and institutions in the province, as well as the explicit costs, opportunity costs, and efficiency losses that are associated with the excessive levels and rates of adjustment that this high degree of variability entails.

The focus of this chapter is on the question, what policies can and should be pursued to reduce this instability and its related costs? Based on the foregoing analysis of the Alberta economy's downturn in the early 1980s, as well as of its fundamental strengths and the sources of its variability generally, we shall outline and evaluate four main policy approaches.

The chapter begins by summarizing the results of a survey of Albertans regarding their attitudes to economic instability and to the policies aimed at reducing it. Then, after outlining the main elements of a solution to the problem, we shall present and evaluate various policy approaches, including improvements in regional sectoral and macroeconomic stabilization, industrial diversification, and private-sector stabilization schemes. Our general conclusions are outlined in the Chapter 6.

The Demand for Economic Stabilization

For any policy initiative to be politically viable, there must be public support for the policy's objectives and public acceptance of any costs associated with it. Thus, we set out to discover the public's perceptions of the seriousness of the province's instability problem and their "willingness to pay" to deal with it. A poll of 1,045 Albertans was taken in February and March 1987, as part of the Alberta Area Survey conducted by the Population Research Laboratory at the University of Alberta.

The province was divided into three areas in the sampling design – the city of Edmonton, the city of Calgary, and the remainder of Alberta – with sample sizes of 254, 281, and 510 for the three areas, respectively. Personal interviews were conducted in Edmonton, telephone interviews in Calgary and the rest of the province. For a survey of this size, results are correct to within four percentage points 19 times out of 20.

The survey, undertaken by the Population Research Laboratory, consisted of 11 different question areas, including a component dealing with the demographic and economic characteristics of the sample. The Western Centre for Economic Research supplied six of the questions for the question area dealing with the Alberta economy. The responses to these questions, in conjunction with the data on the demographic and economic characteristics of the respondents, provided an ideal base from which to assess Albertans' attitudes and responses to instability and diversification. The six questions were posed in a sequence that, it is hoped, prompted the respondents to think in terms of the links among industrial structure, market forces, and government policies that shape the Alberta economic environment.

In order to make the questions as easy to understand as possible, diversification was used to typify stabilization, and reduced average incomes were postulated as the cost of diversification. In reality, of course, diversification is but one of several approaches that can be used to achieve greater stability, and it is not clear that it necessarily entails a reduced standard of living. For the purposes of the survey, however, these generalizations were functional, representing, in essence, the issues that face the public in the matter regarding economic stabilization.

The first question addressed the issue of responsibility for Alberta's poor economic performance, both in terms of absolute indicators and relative to other regions of the country at the time the Alberta Area Survey was undertaken.

1. The Alberta economy is not doing as well as those of Ontario and Quebec. Which of the following do you think is the most responsible for our poor economic condition?

    Market Forces (causing low prices for

    Provincial energy and agricultural products)   26.5%

    Federal Government policies   36.4%

    Provincial Government policies   16.3%

    Poor Business Decisions by Alberta Firms   5.1%

    Trade policies of our major international trading partners   15.7%

This question was asked at a time when agricultural prices were in free fall (as the main participants in the agricultural-subsidy dispute – the European Economic Community and the United States – fought for market share by lowering prices) and when oil prices had touched $10 (U.S.) a barrel. Yet despite the obvious fact that these major shocks to the Alberta economy originated outside Canada, the federal government, rather than market forces, was assigned responsibility for the poor performance of the provincial economy by the majority of the respondents. This perception was, of course, related in part to the hostility that still lingered over the NEP and the view that federal government policies favored central Canada at the expense of the West. Furthermore, it is likely that many of the respondents were thinking not only of the 1986 downturn, but of the economic difficulties that had prevailed throughout the post-1980 period. The ranking of causes provided by the respondents is generally consistent with the diagnosis of Alberta's downturn provided in chapter 3.

The respondent's choices tended to differ depending on their economic and demographic characteristics. For example, individuals who believed market forces were most responsible for Alberta's poor economic performance tended to have higher incomes than those who chose federal government policies or international trading partners'-policies: of those who chose market forces, 59 percent had incomes in excess of $20,000, compared with 43 percent and 36 percent for those who choose trade policies and federal-government policies, respectively. There was also a high correlation between income and educational level among respondents who chose the market-force option – almost 30 percent had university degrees (the percentages of university graduates who chose the remaining four options were 9, 18, 14, and 19, respectively). Location was also a relevant factor. The effect of the agricultural-subsidy dispute had clearly had a impact on

Albertans living outside Calgary and Edmonton – 58 percent of the respondents who chose the trade policies of major trading partners as the cause of Alberta's poor performance lived outside the two major urban centers.

The next question related to the determinants of provincial industrial structure and the notion of specialization:

2. The Alberta economy is highly specialized in the production of oil, natural gas, and agricultural goods for export to other provinces and nations. Which of the following do you think is most responsible for this specialization in oil, gas, and agriculture?

Market forces (and our resource base)	39.3%
Federal government policies	23.7%
Provincial government policies	37.0%

(of 932 respondents to this question, 113 "do not know," etc.; the proportions given are based on the positive responses.)

A small majority of respondents believed that market forces determined industrial structure in Alberta. One somewhat surprising result was the large percentage of respondents who viewed the provincial government as bearing responsibility for the high degree of specialization in the economy. Also, an obvious difference in people's perceptions of the role of the federal government became evident when the responses to questions 1 and 2 were compared. Albertans could be characterized as believing the federal government unfavourably **distorts** the market signals transmitted to the Alberta economy (q. 1), attributing a less important role in determining industrial structure (q. 2). To the extent that government is perceived as a potential agent of change in industrial structure at all, it is the provincial rather the federal government that is seen as the major player. As in question 1, respondents who chose market forces as the factor most responsible for Alberta's industrial structure tended to have a higher income and level of education than did those who chose other options.

The third question of the survey focused directly on the possible trade-off between economic specialization and stability and, as such, sought to determine Albertans' opinions about the **costs** of specialization.

3. Some claim that this economic specialization in Alberta is desirable because it is efficient and leads to higher incomes. Others argue that specialization is not desirable because incomes and employment, while higher on average, are less stable. Which view do you agree with?

Economic specialization in Alberta is desirable because it is efficient and leads to higher incomes.   26.4%

Economic specialization in Alberta is not desirable because incomes and employment, while higher on average, are less stable.   73.6%

(143 respondents replied "Do not know," etc.; the percentages given are based on the positive responses.)

The respondents' overwhelming rejection of specialization, despite the clear link made in the question between it and higher incomes, brings to light Albertans' concerns about instability and its consequences. Three-quarters of the respondents were willing to forgo current income to achieve a more stable income stream. It is the instability arising from specialization that Albertans view as undesirable – most individuals are risk averse and would prefer a lower but more stable income to a higher but riskier one. It is interesting to note that education and income levels and most other economic and demographic variables did **not** differ significantly between the two groups of respondents. Taken together, the responses to questions 2 and 3 suggest why successive provincial governments in Alberta have viewed diversification strategies as an essential element of their economic policies. The electorate clearly views economic specialization as costly and, since it deems the provincial government responsible for the existing pattern of industrial structure, looks to it to propose solutions. Diversification strategies, often involving efforts to broaden the industrial base, have in many cases been the policy response. In the following sections, however, we argue that the problem and the consequences of instability should be addressed directly, by making the macroeconomic environment more stable and thereby mitigating the consequences of instability.

The fourth question explored Albertans' willingness to pay higher taxes in order to finance diversification programs. In light of the response to question 3 and the apparent willingness of respondents to trade off higher income for a more stable income flow, it would seem reasonable to predict that they would also be willing to pay higher taxes to promote diversification. The results, however, proved this assumption wrong.

4. One way to diversify the economy is to provide tax breaks and
    subsidies to industries to develop new activities. How much of a
    percentage increase in your annual taxes would you be willing to pay
    to finance this diversification?

    VALUE

0	58.5%
1 – 4	18.8%
5 – 10	20.7%
11 – 100	2.0%

    (133 respondents replied "did not know etc."; the percentages are
    based on the positive replies.)

While Albertans are apparently willing to sacrifice some of their
standard of living to achieve greater economic stability, they are evidently
less interested paying higher taxes to provide tax breaks and subsidies to
new industries – almost 59 percent of the respondents were unwilling to pay
any additional taxes for this purpose. But, caution should be exercised in
interpreting this result. It is not clear whether it represents an unwillingness
to pay for greater stability or disagreement about the instrument to be
employed. Another possibility is that, for many individuals, economic
stability is a public good, to which they will contribute only if everyone else
makes a similar contribution.[1] In any case, the responses to questions 3 and 4
illustrate the problem facing Alberta governments: the public demands
policies that deal with economic instability, yet is largely unwilling, for a
variety of possible reasons, to provide government with the necessary funds
for the purpose.

The two remaining questions in the survey sought to determine how
Albertans would respond to loss of employment, a variable that was shown
to be far more unstable in Alberta than in other provinces. The responses
offered insight into two related questions:

1. When jobs are lost, do Albertans seek employment outside the province or
    in other sectors within the provincial economy?

2. How much are Albertans willing to "invest," by way of accepting a lower
    income, to remain in the province?

---

1. This phenomenon is called the "isolation paradox" and is common to situations involving a
    public good.

Taken together, the responses to these two questions would provide some indication of the extent to which market-induced diversification, as discussed in chapter 3, might be a plausible outcome during economic downturns.

5. If you lost your job in the coming year, and were unable to find the same kind of job in the same industry, would you

    leave Alberta in search of employment or business opportunities?   16.5%

    seek work in different industry or occupation, but remain in Alberta?   61.7%

    set up your own small business in Alberta?   14.1%

    leave the labor force, but remain in Alberta?   7.7%

    (408 respondents replied "Do not know," etc.; the percentages given are based on positive replies.)

The timing of the survey was partly responsible for the small proportion of respondents who would leave Alberta in response to job loss. Had it been taken in 1982, the number of potential interprovincial migrants would undoubtedly have been higher. The downturn in construction activity accompanying the 1982 slump led to the large-scale outmigration that was discussed in chapter 3. By 1987, many of the younger, economically active workers, especially males employed in construction, had already left the province. Nevertheless, these results suggest that Albertans have a strong preference for remaining in the province in the event of job loss.

The option of seeking work in a different region of the province or in a different occupation, often necessitates a degree of flexibility in wage expectations. The sixth question focused on this issue.

6. How much of a **percentage** cut in your annual income would you be willing to take to change careers or jobs, or to set up your own small business?

Value

0	32.3%
1 – 5	8.4%
6 – 10	21.5%
11 – 30	26.6%
31 – 50	9.9%
51 – 100	1.3%

(488 respondents replied "Do not know," etc.; the percentages given are based on the positive replies.)

More than two-thirds of the respondents would accept a cut in income to regain employment, and almost 60 percent would take a cut in excess of 5 percent. The responses to questions 5 and 6 are clearly consistent with the evidence given in chapter 3 regarding market-based diversification during economic slumps – that is, the Alberta labor market can effect automatic adjustments that promote diversification, but those adjustments will come into play only when the economy is performing badly. Moreover, elements of this market-based diversification are probably only transitory. Once the economy begins to improve and public pressure for wage increases reasserts itself, the tendency toward crowding-out will again promote greater specialization. Only in the case of workers who opt to set up their own small businesses is the diversification prompted by market downturns likely to persist into the next economic upswing.

Although there is considerable room for interpretation, the survey results do seem to mirror three main themes. First, most Albertans consider the degree of variability of the provincial economy unacceptably high. Second, there is a strong demand to reduce this variability, and most Albertans seem willing to accept some drop in their income level if that is what is required to obtain greater stability. Somewhat fewer appear to be interested in paying higher taxes to promote stabilizing diversification through tax breaks and subsidies for industry. Third, Albertans seem quite willing to adapt, even if this involves a sizable reduction in their annual income: they also reveal a strong preference for remaining in the province to seek alternative employment.

These results are interesting not because they are surprising, but because they confirm that the public deems the province's instability problem as serious, wants policies that will deal with it, and shows a willingness to adapt and make sacrifices, if necessary, to achieve greater stability.

Elements of a Solution

It is commonly believed that Alberta's extreme variability is attributable to its resource-based economy and the general instability of resource prices and markets, and that the solution must therefore lie in diversification of the economic base. But the results presented in chapters 3 and 4 clearly indicate that there is considerably more to both the problem and the solution. We demonstrated for example, that the collapse of the Alberta economy in the early 1980s had little to do with the inherent instability of the province's key energy and agricultural sectors. Similarly, the unexpected strength of the economy following the collapse of grain and oil prices in 1986 proved to be largely attributable to shifts in fiscal policy. In short, it became evident that much of Alberta's economic instability stemmed from factors other than its industrial structure, and that these factors would have to be addressed if the variability was to be significantly reduced.

Sector-Specific Policies

As indicated in chapter 3, the NEP played a role in destabilizing and deflating the province's oil and gas industry in the early 1980s. Because the investment and rents associated with this industry represent key driving forces in the overall provincial economy, this naturally led to overall destabilization. It was also shown that, after 1986, the substantial fiscal injections to the agricultural sector, as well as injections to the energy sector through reductions in net royalties, the elimination or reduction of various punitive taxes introduced with the NEP, and various direct-assistance programs, played a major role in reducing the negative impacts associated with the collapse of grain and oil prices. Hence, it is apparent that sector-specific policies can be a major source of both instability and stability.

Given this, it is evident that the first step in reducing Alberta's economic variability must be the avoidance of policies such as the NEP that serve to increase or accentuate any inherent instability in the province's key resource sectors. The second step is to promote sector-specific policies, such as those generally associated with agriculture, that reduce, or compensate for, the inherent instability in particular sector. Sector-specific stabilization policies are generally a practical and cost-effective substitute for the diversification of a narrow, resource-based economy; that is, rather than attempting to change or restructure Alberta's economic base, the initial emphasis should be on policies that reduce the inherent instability of the energy and agriculture sectors.

Macroeconomic Policies

We suggested earlier that Alberta's economic difficulties, especially since the early 1980s, could also be traced to a factor that normally tends to be largely overlooked – namely, the substantial net fiscal surpluses that the federal government has consistently run with the province (while running a net fiscal deficit with every other region). Thus, the tax and expenditure policies of the federal government have continually served to deflate the Alberta economy, while providing a significant economic stimulus to the other regions, including those enjoying prosperity and rapid growth. Although there has been a reduction in the net federal fiscal surplus with Alberta in recent years, it has been stabilizing only in the very narrow sense that the accompanying deflationary impacts on the overall provincial economy have decreased. It seems clear that the elimination of this perverse approach could play a significant role in achieving greater economic stability in Alberta.

The results summarized in chapter 3 also highlight the importance of provincial fiscal policy in reducing the variations that occur in Alberta's economy as a result of external factors such as fluctuations in primary product prices. Two main weaknesses must be addressed, however, if provincial fiscal policies are to be fully effective as a stabilization tool. The first is related to the lack of coordination between federal and provincial fiscal policies. It was noted, for example, that much of the stimulus created by the provincial government's fiscal deficits since 1982 has been drained off to other regions through the federal government's large net fiscal surpluses with Alberta. Thus, for a provincial fiscal deficit to provide a significant stimulus to the regional economy, the federal government must ensure, at a minimum, that it will not remove more from the region in taxes than it returns in expenditures and transfers. A corresponding balance would be required if a provincial fiscal surplus were to be used to dampen growth in the region.

The extreme variability of the Alberta government's revenue base and the impact this has on provincial-government expenditures constitute the second weakness that demands correction. Because of its heavy dependence on royalties and other energy-related revenues, the province's revenue base is particularly vulnerable to fluctuations in energy prices. As it was demonstrated in 1986-87, a downturn in energy prices can result in a dramatic decline in provincial government revenues, to the point where other taxes must be raised, and expenditures cut, even though such actions are entirely counterproductive to stabilizing an economy already reeling from low primary-product prices. It is therefore apparent that measures designed to stabilize the provincial government's revenue base, are another essential element in any approach aimed at achieving greater economic stability in Alberta.

The federal government has possessed the capability of making fiscal stabilization payments directly to provincial governments since 1967.[2] The first payments under the program were made to British Columbia in 1984 to compensate for a decline in provincial revenues in 1982-83. While such a stabilization program would seem to be the ideal mechanism through which problems arising from the volatility of provincial resource revenues could be addressed, the scope of the program directly limits its usefulness to the resource-based western Canadian economies.

The year-to-year decline in natural resource revenues must exceed 50 percent in order to qualify for stabilization.[3] This high threshold before provincial natural resource revenue becomes eligible for stabilization was adopted on the grounds that declines in volume of production or in prices of resources were foreseeable and thus should not be covered by stabilization. This justification is not consistent with much of the available evidence indicating large unanticipated swings in natural resource prices.

Alberta has made a stabilization claim of $540 million under the program for the 30 percent drop in provincial revenues in 1986-87. To date (May 1990) the federal government has made an interim payment of $75 million while the remainder of the claim is the object of continued negotiation between the Alberta and Federal governments.

Thus even federal-provincial programs that deal directly with problems of short-term instability appear curiously biased against the stabilization needs of resource-based provincial governments.

Economic Adjustment and Diversification

One of the major strengths of the Alberta economy has been its ability to adjust quickly and effectively to changing circumstances. As outlined in previous chapters, its unexpected strength in the face of adversity can be attributed in large part to the significant adjustments that were made in cost structures; the mobility of the labor force; the high propensity to start new businesses when old ones failed and various forms of market-induced diversification. It follows that an important element in the search for greater

2. Thomas J. Courchene, *Equalization Payments: Past, Present and Future* (Toronto: Ontario Economic Council, 1984) provides a description of the program.

3. Ibid., p. 72.

economic stability must be the creation of policies that enhance the province's tendencies toward efficient adjustment or, at the very least, the avoidance of policies that inhibit them.

The provincial government's diversification initiatives were also noted as an important factor contributing to Alberta's better-than-expected performance in recent years. Although it is difficult to quantify their stabilizing impacts to date, the various programs to promote research and facilitate the start-up and financing of new businesses have undoubtedly played a role in expanding the province's economic base and increasing the potential for future diversification. Perhaps the most visible result of these programs has been the development of the ethane-based petrochemical industry, which has already added an important degree of stability to the provincial economy. The ultimate success of the province's diversification initiatives will depend mainly on the degree to which any newly created industries or activities exhibit negative covariance with the province's key primary sectors. As shown in chapter 4, this important stabilizing characteristic is, at present, distinctly lacking among existing industries in the province.

Policy Approaches

It should be apparent from the foregoing discussion that no single policy can be the panacea for the Alberta economy's instability problem. Rather, the solution lies in policy changes on a number of fronts, and many of these have little to do with the singular diversification solution that is typically advanced. Indeed, diversification is but one of four main elements required to achieve greater stability. The various policy approaches outlined and evaluated in the following sections.

The Confederation Approach

J.Maxwell and C. Pestieau provide a comprehensive review of the sources of economic gain that are created with an economic union such as Confederation.[4] The economic "surplus" associated with Confederation is seen to derive from four basic factors. The first and most important is the greater specialization of labor and the economies of scale that result from the elimination of barriers to interregional output and factor flows. The larger market of the economic union is thought to permit a more efficient allocation of labor and other factors of production among regions and sectors. The

---

4.   J. Maxwell and C. Pestieau, *Economic Realities of Contemporary Confederation* (Toronto: C.D. Howe Institute, 1980), pp. 13-20.

result of this greater specialization is improved productivity and higher real incomes for the regions in aggregate than if each operated as an independent entity.

The second factor contributing to the economic surplus of Confederation is the potential for a pooling of risks at the national level to mitigate the consequences of regional instability arising from economic specialization. This pooling of risks includes interregional insurance and transfer programs, interprovincial labor and capital flows in response to varying economic opportunities, and macroeconomic stabilization policies aimed at specific regions. The ability to pool risks nationally is, in theory, a particularly useful aspect of an economic union. It permits regions to specialize in the areas of production in which they are most efficient, while simultaneously insulating themselves, at least to some extent, from the major cost of specialization – greater variability of income.

The third factor contributing to the economic surplus in the Maxwell-Pestieau framework is the sharing of overhead expenditures on joint projects such as defence and large-scale transportation projects. And the final factor is the potential market power that only an economic union, never an individual region, could possess. Such market power could be used, for example, to increase export prices or reduce import prices, thereby improving the terms of trade faced by the economic union and increasing aggregate real income.

Whether an economic union realizes these potential gains, however, and, more importantly the extent to which the gains (if they exist), are equitably distributed across regions are not such straight-forward issues. The magnitude of the gains to the participants of the economic union depends critically on the next-best set of trading arrangements open to it. For example, if autarchy were the alternative to Confederation for the provinces, the economic surplus would certainly be great. Conversely, if free trade with the United States or, perhaps, multilateral free trade were the next-best alternative for each of the provinces, the economic surplus from Confederation might be small or even negative, depending on the extent of trade diversion in the Canadian economic union.

Equally significant in determining whether Confederation can yield an economic surplus is the degree to which it promotes economic flexibility in response to economic shocks at the regional level. The gains available through economic union result in part from the enhancement of the interregional and intersectoral mobility of labor and capital. Yet the available evidence suggests, at least from the perspective of Western Canada and Alberta, that Confederation fails both to promote responsiveness to market forces and to provide sufficient mechanisms to help offset the risks of specialization.

Indeed, there is an array of federal policies that are apparently aimed at preserving the status quo in terms of the spatial distribution of population and production. We have already noted the adverse effects of the NEP on the Alberta economy. Certainly one effect of the NEP, as well as of the earlier federal energy policies that accompanied rising oil prices in 1974, was to inhibit the natural westward shift of labor and capital that accompanied the sharp rise in energy prices (relative to manufactured prices). Although oil prices have now plummeted from the heights they had reached by 1986, the 12 years of high prices beginning in 1974 seemed to be viewed by the federal government as an obstacle to be overcome more than an opportunity to exploit the resilience of Confederation.

Other federal programs also tend to focus on preserving the status quo in the spatial distribution of population and production. For example, expenditures by the Department of Regional Industrial Expansion are targeted to regional economies in secular decline, with the effect of inhibiting the market tendency to shift economic resources from regions in decline to those that are prospering. Yet it is this very reallocation of labor and capital among regions and sectors in response to secular decline that is an important factor contributing to the economic surplus of Confederation. Similarly, equalization payments, which may be justified on equity grounds, can have significant negative efficiency effects and serve to dissipate a portion of the potential economic surplus of Confederation. What seems to have emerged at the federal level is a focus on policies that militate against the effects of market forces in correcting secular regional decline, at the expense of policies that could counteract cyclical instability at the regional level.

Confederation represents, at least in theory, an effective and efficient mechanism for regional stabilization, in that it allows each region to specialize in its area(s) of comparative advantage – and thereby to maximize regional (and national) per-capita incomes – without suffering the instability that can be associated with specialization. Some of the stabilizing effects may occur naturally, as the various regional economies become increasingly integrated – for example, any income and employment impacts associated with a stimulus, regardless of its geographical location, come to be more widely spread across the regions. More important, however, is the fact that, in this system, the federal government can play a major role in stabilizing the various regional economies through its fiscal transfer functions. When the industry underpinning one region's economy is hit by cyclical or random events, the federal government can engineer compensating fiscal transfers from the regions whose main industries are prospering.

Furthermore, with Confederation, the overall net fiscal balance that the federal government runs with each region would ideally depend on the region's relative economic performance. In a balanced federal budget, for example, the government would run a surplus with the "have" regions and a deficit with the "have-not" regions. In addition, the fiscal balance with each region would vary with that region's economic fluctuations. For example, a "have" region suffering a cyclical downturn would see a decline in its net federal fiscal balance, or and perhaps even a reversal to a deficit position, as the combination of federal tax and expenditure policies worked to produce a net stimulus to the region.

Many of these stabilizing mechanisms do, in fact, exist within the Canadian Confederation. A number of the components of federal-government revenues (such as personal and corporate income taxes) and federal expenditures (such as social assistance and unemployment insurance) vary directly with the economic situations of individuals and, hence, of regions. Indeed, as indicated by the data in Appendix Table A-1, the actual net fiscal balances for most regions seem to correspond quite closely to what the principles of regional equity and stabilization world demand.[5] The balances with Alberta are the gross exception in this regard. It should be noted, however, that the Confederation approach falls short in two important areas with respect to stabilizing the Alberta economy. One concerns the regional trade patterns that have evolved in Canada, while the other has to do with biases intrinsic to energy policy, on the one hand, and discretionary federal spending, on the other.

Alberta, as well as the West in general, relies heavily on international markets for its exports and on domestic (central Canadian) markets for its imports. Consequently, the regional "spread" effects described above tend to run in only one direction. For example, an economic expansion in Alberta results in significant additional economic activity in Ontario, but an expansion in Ontario generates few positive impacts in Alberta.[6] Thus, there is little opportunity for the province to gain stability indirectly, through interregional trade, from the greater inherent stability of the central

---

5. For example, relative to the overall deficit, the per-capita deficits with the lowest-income provinces (such as Newfoundland, New Brunswick, Nova Scotia, and Prince Edward Island) and provinces in a cyclical downturn (such as Saskatchewan and British Columbia) have been larger than those with the higher-income provinces (such as Ontario). As indicated in Appendix Table A-1, Alberta, even with its serious downturn after 1982, remains the only province with which the federal government has continued to run a fiscal surplus.

6. This lack of symmetry is perhaps best illustrated by the interregional impact tables of Statistics Canada, Input-Output Division, *Interprovincial Input-Output Model* (Ottawa: Supply and Services, 1979).

Canadian or other regional economies. Unfortunately, these trade patterns are not easy to change; moreover, to do so would likely involve an unacceptable sacrifice of overall economic welfare.

The second weakness of the Confederation approach is associated with all these factors that lead to destabilizing energy policies, low levels of discretionary federal spending in Alberta, and perverse net federal fiscal balances with the province. Although these causal factors are difficult to measure and disentangle, they appear to be related mainly to a combination of the following: a huge imbalance in federal political power between the net energy-consuming and the net energy-producing regions; endemic economic colonialism; misperceptions about the oil and gas industry; and large regional variations in industrial structure.

The imbalance in political power is well documented[7] and suggests that, in the absence of political reform, the interests of the net energy-consuming provinces will continue to dominate those of Alberta through all phases of energy price cycles. (In this regard, it is appropriate to recall the previously mentioned criticism of the Canada-U.S. Free Trade Agreement on the grounds that it will make reimposing an NEP more difficult.) There are other factors that serve to accentuate this tendency as well.

First, there is the widespread, "Colonial" view that the main purpose of Alberta's oil and gas industry is to provide cheap energy for the industrial heartland, rather than (as in the case of most other industries) to directly and indirectly provide employment and income for many Canadians. Second, the petroleum industry is invariably associated with foreign ownership and control, despite many other key industries, such as Canadian auto manufacturing, having considerably higher levels of foreign ownership and control. And, unlike the oil and gas industry, those industries are not subject to close regulation to ensure that their behavior is consistent with maximizing net benefits for Canada.[8]

Third, there is a distinct duality in government treatment of the oil and gas industry, on the one hand, and other energy industries, on the other. For example, hydroelectricity production in Canada is heavily subsidized, and the substantial economic rents are uncollected and untaxed.[9] The oil and gas

---

7. For example, see P. McCormick, E.C. Manning and G. Gibson, *Regional Representation: The Canadian Partnership* (Calgary: Canada West Foundation, 1981).

8. Such regulation of the Alberta oil and gas industry is carried out by the Energy Resources Conservation Board, the National Energy Board, and various (provincial) Public Utility Boards.

9. For further information on this subject, see R.C. Zuker and G.P. Jenkins, *Blue Gold: Hydro-Electric Rent in Canada*, A Study Prepared for the Economic Council of Canada (Ottawa: Supply and Services, 1984), and G.P. Jenkins, "Public Utility Finance and Economic Waste," *Canadian Journal of Economics* 18 (1985): 484-498.

industry, on the other hand, pays considerable taxes, does not have its debt guaranteed by governments, and has the rents associated with its production collected and distributed by governments.

This also results in an inconsistency in the federal government's treatment of regional fiscal capacities. For example, Alberta is a highly successful collector of energy rents, and this has allowed the province to build up the Alberta Heritage Savings Trust Fund. But the existence of this fund has often been used as justification for subjecting the province to special taxes or giving it a less-than-proportionate share of federal expenditures, or both. By comparison, Ontario and Quebec distribute energy rents through artificially low electricity prices. Since the benefits do not show up in a highly visible fund, they escape notice – and measurement as part of regional fiscal capacity. It is interesting to note that, as of the end of 1986, the combined retained equity of Ontario Hydro and Quebec Hydro alone was $11.7 billion, an amount roughly equal to the financial assets of the Alberta Heritage Savings Trust Fund.[10]

All of these factors, along with the failure to recognize that, in Canada, federal energy policies are in effect regional as much as they are "national" policies, clearly work against the use of sector-specific federal initiatives to help stabilize the province's key energy sector. In addition, they do not augur well for increases in the disproportionately low levels of discretionary federal spending in the province, especially in areas such as procurement and regional and industrial development.[11] Consequently, it is likely that, in the absence of any major policy shifts, the perverse nature of the net federal fiscal balance with respect to Alberta will continue, and will continue to have a deflationary and destabilizing impact on the overall provincial economy.

There is one additional problem with federal policy vis-a-vis Alberta's economic variability. Specifically, it is the recent combination of maintaining fiscal deficits with booming regional economies and imposing a restrictive monetary policy to contain the inflationary pressures emanating from these economies. For example, as noted earlier (see Table A-1), the federal government has been running a large fiscal deficit with Ontario even though the Ontario economy has exhibited exceptional fundamental strength since the latter part of 1983. This significant fiscal stimulus has been further bolstered by the sizable fiscal deficits run by the government of Ontario

10. Data from Ontario Hydro and Quebec Hydro (Annual Reports) and Alberta Heritage Savings Trust Fund (Annual Report, 1986-87).

11. For example, see Canada, *Economic Growth, Services and Subsidies to Business and Management of Government: Procurement*, Reports to the Task Force on Program Review (Ottawa: Supply and Services, 1985).

itself. Thus, we have the spectre of an expansionary fiscal policy contributing to the overheating of the Ontario economy, then a restrictive monetary policy to contain its inflationary tendencies. For a weakened economy like Alberta's, such a combination is extremely damaging. Given the province's capital-intensive, investment-driven nature and the fact that many of its exports are priced in U.S. dollars, the high interest rates and related appreciation of the Canadian dollar (vis-a-vis the U.S. dollar) have very significant deflationary impacts. Contributing further to this deflation is the federal government's sustained net fiscal surplus with Alberta. The net result of these policy combinations for the province is an unfavorable twisting of regional economic performance.

Although the historical, institutional, attitudinal, and political underpinnings of these various factors are unquestionably strong, they **can** be changed and such change should indeed be pursued. At a minimum, this would involve the avoidance of destabilizing policies like the NEP. In costing future energy policies, governments should pay greater attention to their regional impacts and to the elements that add to the variability of the oil and gas sector. Furthermore, if it is uneconomical or politically unacceptable to spread discretionary federal expenditures (in such areas as employment creation, procurement, and regional development) more equitably across the regions, a system of federal rebates could be instituted. For example, a province such as Alberta, which receives a disproportionately small share of these expenditures, could be compensated by an intergovernmental fiscal transfer or a federal tax rebate to the residents of the province.

Finally, an additional step could be added to the federal budgetary process to ensure that the net federal fiscal balances for each region are at least roughly consistent with regional equity and stabilization objectives. This alone could serve to prevent a replay of the situation in Alberta, where the combination of federal tax and expenditure policies has operated to further deflate and destabilize an already weak and unstable economy. An additional benefit of this kind of policy shift would be a reduction not only in actual inequities but in the perception of inequities among the provinces regarding the regional distribution of discretionary federal expenditures.

Regional Balance and Confederation

Perhaps the most contentious issue in any economic union is the distribution of the gains (or losses) from economic integration among the participants. Chapters 3 and 4 of this study have examined the instability of the Alberta economy and the role of federal policies in exacerbating it. The instability might, however, be more acceptable if it were balanced by the perception **and reality** of an equitable distribution of the (ideally) positive economic surplus of Confederation. Unfortunately, the available evidence clearly suggests that residents of Alberta pay a disproportionate share of the "price" of being Canadian. Whalley and Trela, in their research study for the Royal Commission on the Economic Union and Development Prospects for the Future, have constructed a balance sheet of Confederation that illustrates the regional distribution of gains and losses associated with the full array of existing federal and provincial policies.[12]

Balance-sheet exercises are fraught with difficulties, as the authors point out in their study.[13] The estimates used in such studies depend critically on the next-best-alternative trading arrangements specified and the policy framework and international trading environment in place at the time the exercise is undertaken. The Whalley and Trela exercise is based on data and policies for 1981, a period characterized by high oil prices and the NEP. Thus, their results probably overstate significantly the current costs of Confederation to Alberta.

Two aspects of their analysis bear discussion. The first is the result of a general-equilibrium analysis of the impact that regions would experience if major existing federal programs (including the NEP; the federal tariff; intergovernmental transfers; transfers to persons; and federal personal and corporate taxes as well as existing sales taxes) were replaced by a federal sales tax to finance the same level of real expenditure on goods and services. The results are shown in Table 8.

In 1981, then, Alberta evidently stood to gain the most from a shift to a less distorting set of mechanisms for financing real federal expenditures. The major gain to the province would have come from the removal of the NEP. These results also indicate that in 1981, the economic surplus of Confederation was negative. Again, it must be emphasized that these results are sensitive to the year of the study and to the assumptions that were made about next-best-alternative trading arrangements.

The second set of results relevant to our discussion shows the general-equilibrium effects that the withdrawal of various regions from Confederation would have on both the regions that withdraw and those that remain in the economic union (see Table 9). The exercise assumes that no further federal expenditures or tax collections are made in a region that opts out. Any gain or loss to the federal government resulting from the withdrawal of a region is distributed proportionally among the remaining regions on the basis of population weights. Capital is assumed to remain mobile among regions and sectors, but labor is fixed at the regional level.

---

12. Whalley and Trela, *Regional Aspects of Confederation*, pp. 196-200.

13. Ibid., pp. 182-183.

Table 8. General Equilibrium Impact on Canadian Regions
of Replacing Major Existing Federal Programs by a Federal Sales Tax
to Finance Real Expenditures of the Federal Government

($millions,[a] 1981 data)

Atlantic Provinces	$-5,316
Quebec	-6,411
Ontario	-199
Manitoba, Saskatchewan	491
Alberta	15,866
British Columbia	1,093
Total	5,710

[a]Measured in terms of Hicksian equivalent variation.

Source: John Whalley and Irene Trela, *Regional Aspects of Confederation*, Royal Commission on the Economic Union and Development Prospects for Canada, Vol. 68 (Toronto: University of Toronto Press, 1986), table 6.1.

The results of Table 9 are broadly consistent with the evidence on net federal fiscal balances discussed earlier, in chapters 3 and 4. Had Alberta opted out of Confederation in 1981, provincial income would have risen by $20.5 billion, leading to a total decline in income in the remaining five regions of $20 billion. Conversely, had Ontario withdrawn, its income would have risen by $0.7 billion, while the remaining five regions would have experienced a total loss of $5.4 billion. The losses experienced by Alberta as a result of Ontario's opting out of Confederation arise because the scenario assumes that the NEP would remain in place.

Balance-sheet exercises are necessarily speculative, but the Whalley and Trela study is more firmly rooted in theory and in a specific modelling approach than were, for example, any of the earlier balance-sheet exercises undertaken in the debates about sovereignty association for Quebec. It is worth noting Whalley and Trela's conclusions about the implications of their results:

> The theme emerging from these results appears to be that in 1981, at least, Confederation was not the grand compromise depicted by Mackintosh in the 1930s. The major change over this period was the growth in importance of resource rents and the interregional effects produced by federal policies toward them. Thus, Confederation appears to be substantially unbalanced both against resource-rich and higher-income provinces. In addition, these results suggest that, if anything, rather than accounting for a surplus to be

Table 9. General Equilibrium Impacts of
Withdrawal from Confederation by Individual Regions[a]
($ millions,[b] 1981 data)

	Withdrawal by					
Impacts on	Atlantic Provinces	Quebec	Ontario	Man./ Sask.	Alberta	British Columbia
Atlantic provinces	$-5,150	$358	$-512	$-189	$-1,417	$-329
Quebec	607	-6,394	-1,937	-663	-5,674	-1,197
Ontario	792	1,801	713	-1,204	-7,901	-1,943
Manitoba/ Saskatchewan	168	331	-630	1,310	-2,209	-429
Alberta	224	308	-1,154	-751	20,534	-667
British Columbia	208	419	-1,163	-385	-2,875	2,389
Total for six original regions	-3,251	-3,177	-4,683	-1,882	459	-2,176
Total for five remaining regions	1,899	3,217	-5,396	-3,192	-20,076	-4,565

[a]Each of these model experiments is specified by removing intergovernmental transfers and federal transfers to persons in the region, federal taxes paid, and expenditures by the federal government on goods produced by the region. Any gain or loss to the federal government produced by the model has been reallocated to the remaining regions on a proportional basis.

[b]Measured in terms of Hicksian equivalent variation.

Source: Whalley and Trela, *Regional Aspects of Confederation*, table 6.3.

distributed among regions, Confederation seems to account for a deficit, and this seems to be due in large part to the distorting policies pursued by the federal government.[14]

As noted earlier, because the regulatory framework of the NEP has largely been dismantled by the Conservative government since its election in 1984, the regional imbalances indicated in Table 9 are probably greater than they would be today. Unfortunately, the shift to a market-based energy policy coincided with the slump in energy prices, so the West failed to realize many of the anticipated benefits of the Western Accord. Perhaps even more disturbing, however, is the notion that the removal of the NEP is sufficient to address Alberta's concerns about fairness in the regional balance of Confederation – the multibillion-dollar cost of the NEP to the

14. Ibid., pp. 199.

energy-producing provinces is viewed as a bygone. Moreover, the policy
framework that has emerged under the federal Conservatives continues to
ignore the issue of cyclical instability, the Western Diversification Fund
notwithstanding. This point will be developed in greater detail in our
analysis of diversification policies, later in the chapter.

The Provincial Stabilization Approach

Sector-Specific Policies

Provincial-government fiscal and sector-specific policies can be and have
been effective tools for stabilizing the Alberta economy. Indeed, as
demonstrated in Chapter 3, such policies were by far the most important
factor contributing to the unexpected strength of Alberta's economy
following the collapse of oil and grain prices. Moreover, because the
potential for improvement in the realization of the Confederation approach
is severely limited by political factors, the main responsibility for stabilizing
the economy will likely remain with the provincial government. The key
question, then, is What types of changes can be made to increase the
effectiveness of provincial stabilization policies?

As noted earlier, variations in energy investment and, to a lesser extent,
variations in agricultural incomes have contributed substantially to the
overall instability of the Alberta economy. The importance of provincial
policies aimed at stabilizing these components is therefore obvious.
Although we cannot examine or evaluate all of the main alternatives within
the scope of this study, a number of general observations can usefully be
made.

Many of the important determinants of energy investment (for example,
energy prices, expectations with respect to future prices, export-market
access, and the cost of debt – equity capital) are beyond the control of the
provincial government. But the province can exert significant influence
through its control over variables such as royalty rates, holidays and tax
credits, and direct investment incentives, as well as through its approval
process for megaprojects. Provincial policies in these areas can contribute to
greater stability in energy investment by ensuring consideration of the
following critical elements:

1. **A greater emphasis on the long run**. That is, policies in these areas should
   encourage firms to base their investment decisions on longer-term economic
   fundamentals rather than on short-run fluctuations and extrapolations from
   them. In other words, policies that encourage firms, for example, to incur
   high debt-equity ratios in the pursuit of short-run investment opportunities

should be avoided. In addition, royalty rates should be made not only to adjust in line with cyclical variations in energy prices and rents[15] but also to average out, over the longer term, to the levels consistent with optimal rates of depletion.

2. **A greater appreciation of the general-equilibrium effects of policy shifts.** For example, programs such as the Alberta Royalty Tax Credit can be effective in encouraging investment by the smaller producers. But in an environment of deregulated oil and gas prices, the resulting decline in these prices can reduce the net-backs of other producers and thereby generate offsetting declines in their investment expenditures.[16] Thus, when the general-equilibrium effects are considered, it is not at all clear that the objective of stabilizing overall energy investment is being achieved. If, on the other hand, the purpose is to alter the distribution of energy investment and activity (for example, between small and large producers), other types of programs, such as those based on insurance principles, may be more effective and less destabilizing for the overall energy sector.

3. **Greater attention to the timing and scheduling of energy megaprojects.** In many cases, the construction requirements of energy megaprojects are much too large to be accommodated by the province's construction sector and other input-providing sectors at their normal capacities. A "stacking" for such projects can therefore ensue, resulting, first, in an overexpansion of these sectors, and then, once construction is completed, in substantial overcapacity. Although it may not be possible to select the timing of such projects, it may be possible to mitigate their effects through more effective planning, the use of the approval process, and, perhaps, the use of financial incentives to alter construction patterns and timing.

In the case of the agriculture sector, a variety of federal and provincial programs aimed at stabilization are already in place. Nevertheless, there is undoubtedly room for further modifications or new programs. It might be possible to devise a more broadly based insurance scheme, for example, that

---

15. That is, net royalty rates would be increased during a cyclical or random upturn in energy prices to prevent the capitalization of the higher rents in the form of rapidly escalating input costs. Conversely, in a downturn, royalty rates would be reduced to avoid a situation where collections exceeded 100 percent of the rents and, consequently, where energy investment would be artificially depressed.

16. This is particularly true in natural gas markets, where incremental supplies of low- or zero-royalty gas serve to reduce the prices received on all volumes of gas sold into the market.

would allow farmers to purchase protection against cyclical or random fluctuations in agriculture prices.

Sector-specific initiatives that influence the timing of public-works projects can also play a significant role in stabilizing the provincial economy. Investment expenditures on transportation and other utilities, together with capital expenditures by government departments, typically account for between 20 percent and 25 percent of total investment in the province.[17] Moreover, as demonstrated earlier (see Table 7), the province's construction sector is the single most variable sector in Alberta and considerably more variable than its counterparts in other regions. It is therefore apparent that any initiative by the provincial government to make investment expenditures in these areas conform to a more anticyclical pattern would undoubtedly add a significant degree of stability to the Alberta economy.

Provincial Fiscal Policies

Our focus until now has been on sector-specific policies. But the aggressive use of anticyclical provincial fiscal policy represents an equally important component of economic stabilization. In general, the objective here is to reduce provincial taxes and/or increase expenditures in a downturn (beyond the reductions in taxes and increases in expenditures that automatically occur when income falls) and engage the reverse combination of tax and expenditure shifts as the economy approaches full employment.

A distinct lack of symmetry is evident, especially in Alberta, in the use of such policy shifts to flatten and extend economic upturns and to fill in troughs. It may be politically difficult to reduce expenditures and increase taxes as fiscal surpluses accumulate during an upturn, but there are no practical or economic limitations to doing so. In fact, the very existence of the Alberta Heritage Savings Trust Fund (AHSTF) makes such a shift easier to accomplish in Alberta than in most other regions. In a downturn, however, while fewer political difficulties would surround the opposite fiscal-policy shift, very serious fiscal constraints would come into play, especially if the downturn were associated with declining energy prices or production. In this case, the rapid and substantial drops in provincial-government revenues and the resulting ballooning of the fiscal deficit would make it extremely difficult to embark on stimulative tax-and expenditure-policy shifts. Rather, as evidenced by recent experience, the response is more likely to be a destabilizing combination of higher taxes and reductions in expenditures.

---

17. Alberta Bureau of Statistics, *Alberta Statistical Review* (various issues), table 39.

Revenue Stabilization

It is readily apparent that, in order to increase the ability of the province to follow an aggressive countercyclical fiscal policy, as well as to pursue many of the sector-specific stabilization policies noted earlier, the provincial government's revenue base must be made more stable. Although additional taxes could be introduced to broaden the revenue base, a more effective approach would involve attacking the real source of the problem – the instability of the resource-revenue components – directly. What is required, then, is a mechanism to convert a highly variable income flow into a stable one.

As perhaps best demonstrated by the AHSTF, one such mechanism would involve accumulating (unstable) resource revenues in a capital fund, then channelling the (more stable) flow of interest and dividend income into the General Revenue Account. A Revenue Stabilization Fund would have to be established, perhaps in combination with the AHSTF, and a commitment made to flow a fixed percentage (say, 30 percent or 40 percent) of all future royalty revenue, after a given transition period, into this fund. Furthermore, all of these revenues would have to be invested in a diversified portfolio of financial assets, and the resulting investment income transferred annually into the General Revenue Account. Great care must be taken, however, in the design of a Revenue Stabilization Fund to ensure that it, too, does not ultimately contribute to instability. Recent work by R. Pollock and J. P. Suyderhoud has shown that formula-based rainy day funds can indeed be destabilizing if they are not properly implemented.[18]

It should be emphasized that the Revenue Stabilization Fund, unlike the AHSTF, would contain no "deemed assets." In fact, this approach would indirectly involve the elimination of deemed assets from AHSTF accounting.[19] In general, deemed assets create a misleading picture of the overall fiscal strength of the province and ultimately contribute to its unfair treatment under federal tax and expenditure programs.[20]

---

18. Richard Pollock and Jack P. Suyderhoud, "The Role of Rainy Day Funds in Achieving Fiscal Stability," *National Tax Journal* 39 (1986): 485-497.

19. A case can be made for including deemed assets that increase future productive capacity (such as investments in education and infrastructure), along with liabilities (debt) in public-sector accounting. It can indeed be argued that a failure to include "productive expenditures" results in a distorted view of the "burden" of public debt. This is really no different from the distortion that would exist in private-sector accounting if liabilities, but not assets, were counted. The fact remains, however, that public-sector accounting does not include deemed assets, and it does not make sense to confuse the issue by including them in AHSTF accounting.

20. As noted earlier, there already exists a bias in this regard. For example, equity in a fund such as the AHSTF is highly visible, while equivalent equity in, say, Ontario Hydro and Quebec Hydro is not.

Corporate Tax Reform

Another vehicle for addressing the issue of instability and dealing with its consequences is reform of the corporate tax system. A corporate tax system that uses a cash-flow base has characteristics that make it both an efficient tax framework and one that is particularly well suited to an unstable economy such as Alberta's.[21] An efficient tax regime is one that captures a significant share of economic profits without discriminating against the marginal investment that yields no more than the market rate of return. Economic profits differ from accounting profits in that the former represent returns over and above the market rate of return. The current tax system has a number of distortions that may in fact exacerbate the inherent instability of the Alberta economy.

The current tax system discourages investments in risky activities – profits are heavily taxed, while losses are not subsidized by the government. Although the corporate tax system does permit the deduction of losses, it does not allow for full loss refundability. Losses cannot be carried forward indefinitely and the forgone income on the losses is ignored by the tax system entirely. (At any rate, firms may not survive the losses to apply them against future profits). Such asymmetry in the tax treatment of profits and losses is acutely felt in an unstable economy. J. M. Mintz has calculated that the current tax regime imposes a very high effective tax rate on new or start-up investments.[22]

A cash-flow corporate tax system would allow for full expensing of investments (with no interest deductibility or depreciation against profits) and full loss offset; in short, it would apply high effective tax rates on economic profits and low rates on marginal investments. Such a system does not discriminate against risky start-up investments. Also, the shift to a cash-flow base would be accompanied by several desirable administrative features. Because cash-flow is readily observable, informational problems in this base are relatively small. The shift to a cash-flow base, with full expensing for investments and full refundability of losses, would also do away with problematic information requirements for deductions such as interest payments and depreciation.

21. See Robin Boadway, Neil Bruce, and Jack Mintz, "Corporate Taxation in Canada: Towards an Efficient System," in *Tax Policy Options in the 1980s*, ed. Wayne Thirsk and John Whalley (Toronto: Canadian Tax Foundation, 1982), pp. 171-216, and J.M. Mintz and Douglas D. Purvis, "Economic Instability: What Is the Appropriate Government Response?" (Paper presented at the conference Unstable Commodity Markets: Incomes, Jobs, and Public Policy, Calgary, Alberta, April 13-14, 1988).

22. J.M. Mintz, "An Empirical Estimate of Corporate Tax Refundability and Effective Tax Rates," *Quarterly Journal of Economics* 103 (1988): 225-232.

Perhaps the greatest attraction of a cash-flow corporate tax system for a province such as Alberta is that it is inherently countercyclical. During periods of slack economic activity, the cash-flow position of firms declines, as, consequently, do corporate taxes accruing to government. The full-loss-offset provisions also act as a stimulus for firms caught in unanticipated downturns. Similarly, during upswings in economic activity, the corporate tax revenues of government rise proportionately, and thereby moderate the magnitude of the cycle.

From the perspective of the Alberta government, there are three potential problems with a cash-flow tax system. In order of increasing importance, they are

1. the transition,

2. the revenue position of government, and

3. interface with the federal system.

Any shift in government tax policies usually imposes a range of costs on existing taxpayers. Firms have undertaken investments on the assumption that the "rules of the game" governing taxes are stable. And since most corporate investments are very long-term, the present value of various anticipated deductions is a significant determinant of investment activity. The shift to a new tax regime would therefore require either that activities undertaken during the original regime be governed by the original rules or, if possible, that the government pay out the present value of depreciation and write-off obligations under the original regime.

It is costly to undertake significant policy changes in the realm of taxation. But, the costs of change must be weighed against the potential benefits – in this case, those of a corporate tax regime that does not discriminate against risk-taking activity and that is inherently more countercyclical than the existing tax regime. A shift to a cash-flow tax system might have a significant negative impact on the fiscal capacity of the provincial government in the short term; full loss offset and full expensing would lead to a reduction in government revenues and an increase in expenditures. In the longer term, however, government revenues would increase, because deductions for interest payments and depreciation against profits would no longer be permitted. Moreover, to the extent that the shift to a cash-flow regime would increase the volume of investments by removing discrimination against risky start-up investments and smoothing out economic cycles, the expansion of the tax base might actually increase government tax revenues.

The greatest difficulty facing any one province in shifting to a corporate tax system based on cash-flow is the integration of its corporate tax regime with the current federal system. Indeed, it seems unlikely that one province alone could opt for a cash-flow system, while the other provinces and the federal government maintained the existing regime. The cost to firms of dealing with two different tax regimes would be high and many of the beneficial effects of a cash-flow regime adopted by a single province would be offset to some extent by the federal tax regime. On the other hand, the costs of the current system are relatively high in Alberta, in light of the nature of its economy. One possible strategy might be to introduce a cash-flow tax system in only one or two of the province's cyclically most unstable sectors – such as energy or agriculture.

Personal Tax Reform
We noted earlier that it is highly likely that the labor market suffers from some degree of market failure. Workers cannot diversify their sources of labor income in response to risk. Moreover, the costs to labor of adjusting to a risky environment are high, and are often not reflected in prevailing market wage rates. In particular, migration is sometimes not an efficient response to shocks affecting a provincial economy, especially if those shocks are short term. Large swings in net migration prompted by transitory shocks tend to exacerbate the economic variability associated with resource-price swings. One objective of the personal tax system should be to smooth out short-term swings in the taxable income of Alberta residents.

If, for example, provincial personal tax payments (not income) were averaged over two or three years, the tax burden on Alberta residents, particularly during downturns, would be lessened. Consider the case of a worker who has been fully employed, but suddenly finds himself without employment for a portion of the year. Since his income for the current year has fallen, so too has his tax payable. Under a tax-averaging policy, however, the worker could apply some of the taxes paid in preceding years to his current (lower) personal tax liability. The net effect would be to increase workers' disposable income when it is most required. The provisions of such a program would come into effect only if the personal tax liability of a worker was lower in the current year than in the preceding one. This "ratchet" would ensure that such a program would only come into effect during periods of declining economic activity and not during upswings.

Such a program has a number of desirable features in light of the volatility of the Alberta economy. First, it can come into effect automatically and is inherently countercyclical, as it increases disposable incomes, during

downturns but not during upswings. Second, it naturally restricts itself to
Alberta residents, since the plan can only benefit those who have paid at
least one year's personal taxes to the Alberta government. Such a program
might usefully be viewed as an "investment" in Alberta residents to enable
them to weather short-term shocks. Moreover, by limiting the tax averaging
to a period of two or three years and by imposing the constraint that the
current tax liability must be lower than that of the preceding year, the
program deals with only short-term fluctuations in economic activity. With
regard to permanent, or long-term shifts, government policy should aim to
promote interregional adjustment and interprovincial migration. Personal
tax policies such as the one suggested here would ameliorate adjustment to
short-term instability without inhibiting the long-run adjustment of the
provincial economy to permanent shocks.

The Diversification Approach

Unlike other approaches aimed at altering economic flows, industrial
diversification represents an attempt to change the structure of the regional
economy – and herein lie both its political attractiveness and its practical
difficulties. It is invariably attractive because of the broad public support that
can be relied upon for the new and "better" industries it promises and
because, to the extent that new industries do materialize, they represent
tangible and highly visible evidence of policy results. The practical
difficulties arise because, even under the best of circumstances, regional
economic structures are not easily changed – and the time it takes to achieve
significant structural change is typically measured in decades rather than
years and invariably extends beyond the planning and policy horizon of
most governments. Added to this is the fact that diversification is inherently
difficult to define and measure and, thus, diversification strategies, like
industrial-development strategies, tend to be vague and difficult to put into
operation. Finally, structural change can be extremely expensive, especially
when it clashes with market realities.

Rationale for Diversification Strategies

Neither the extensive public support for diversification initiatives nor the
high degree of instability discussed in chapter 4 constitutes a strong case for
government intervention to diversify the Alberta economy by altering its
industrial structure. A case for direct government intervention in an
economy can be made when there is clear evidence of "market failure."
Market failure is said to exist when market prices fail to reflect the costs and

benefits to society of activities undertaken by individuals and firms. Under these circumstances, government intervention actually increases real income and improves economic efficiency.

The existence of instability is, in fact, a common justification for direct intervention. Yet, under ideal conditions, freely functioning markets have the capacity to deal adequately with risk. For example, workers in industries characterized by bouts of unemployment may insist on higher wages during periods of employment in order to equalize their expected income (including risk premiums) with that of more stable industries. Similarly, investors often may demand higher returns on capital invested is risky industries as compensation for possible loss. Moreover, investors can often spread their investments across a portfolio of risky and safe investments to protect themselves against potential losses.

Of course, few markets are perfect. Labor markets, in particular, may be characterized by a high degree of market failure. It is virtually impossible for a worker to diversify his sources of income; in most instances, the income that derives from physical skills and human capital (education) is the sole source of income. Furthermore, lack of information may also make it very difficult for workers to evaluate the inherent riskiness of employment in a particular industry (by comparison, investors are far better informed). Finally, the financial and psychological costs of responding to uncertain market opportunities can cause many profitable options for interregional and intersectoral labor reallocation to remain unrealized. Conversely, such costs can cause labor to stay locked into industries in which the departure of workers would be the more appropriate response.

Instability can thus lead to market failure and thereby warrant government intervention. Yet it is not at all clear that diversification (in the sense of altering industrial structure in favor of more stable industries) is the appropriate response – it may, in fact, exacerbate the problem of instability, because the growth it promotes may not be sustainable during periods of declining economic activity. One of a number of themes that will emerge in the following discussion is that treating the consequences of instability directly, through more appropriate risk-sharing programs and better information, may be a more effective response.

This is not to suggest that policies aimed at diversifying the economy cannot or should not form an important component of the overall attempt to stabilize the Alberta economy. Rather, it is to emphasize that, if a diversification strategy is to be effective, it must include the following:

1. a clear definition of the diversification objective;

2. a recognition of the limitations and costs of diversification policies;

3. consistent and sustained policy initiatives over a long period of time;

4. policies aimed at correcting or compensating for market imperfections, rather than at attempting to change fundamental market economics.

Meaning of Diversification

In order to devise an effective diversification strategy, it is first necessary to have a clear, operational definition of diversification. Unfortunately, there appears to be much confusion in this regard, which stems in part from a failure to distinguish among the various types of instability that diversification is intended to reduce. In some cases, diversification is aimed at reducing secular instability arising, for example, from the depletion of the region's resource base, while in others, its objective is to reduce seasonal or cyclical instability.[23] Since this study focuses on cyclical and random instability, we can at least dispel any confusion that may exist about these two types.

A number of conceptual problems in defining and measuring diversification, remain, however, and these have yet to be resolved in the literature on this topic.[24] Much of the difficulty stems from the fact that

---

23. For example, Alberta's diversification strategy, which originated in the mid-1970s, emphasized secular stability and the need to "become less dependent on the sale of unprocessed resources" (Premier's Policy Statement, *Alberta Hansard*, October 23, 1974, pp. 3133-3134). But most of the literature on diversification focuses on structural change designed to reduce a regional economy's vulnerability to general economic cycles. See, for example, John R. Kort "Regional Economic Instability and Industrial Diversification in the U.S.," *Land Economics* 57 (1981): 596-608. Also, in most cases, the type of structural change needed to reduce, say, cyclical instability would differ from that needed to decrease, say, seasonal or secular instability.

24. For a summary of the various definitions and measures of regional industrial diversification, see M.E. Conroy, "The Concept and Measurement of Regional Industrial Diversification" and also Charles B. Garrison and Albert S. Paulson, "An Entropy Measure of the Geographic Concentration of Economic Activity," *Economic Geography* 49 (1973): 319-324; M.J. Wasylenko and R.A. Erickson, "On Measuring Economic Diversification: Comment," *Land Economics* 54 (1978): 106-110; J.R. Kort, "Regional Economic Instability and Industrial Diversification in the U.S'"; H.L. Brewer and Ronald L. Moomaw, "A Note on Population Size, Industrial Diversification and Regional Economic Instability," *Urban Studies* 22 (1985): 349-354; and H.L. Brewer, "Measures of Diversification: Predictions of Regional Economic Instability," *Journal of Regional Science* 25 (1985): 463-470. It might also be noted that the presence of an empirical relationship between stability and diversity seems to depend heavily on the particular measure of diversification being used.

diversification, especially as it relates to regional economic stability, is a multidimensional concept. Four of the more important of these dimensions are

1. diversity with respect to industrial structure;

2. diversity of markets;

3. diversity in the range of commodities produced by existing industries; and

4. the degree of processing of raw materials in the region.

The relationship between stability and industrial composition is most easily seen the context of financial portfolio theory. For example, in the simple case of two assets, **A** and **B**, the variability of the portfolio will be Var (**A**+**B**) = Var(**A**) + Var(**B**) + 2Covariance(**AB**). Using this analogy, the instability of a regional economy depends on the variability of each of its industrial sectors and the extent to which they tend to move together (positive covariance) or in opposite directions (negative covariance). Thus, to stabilize the economy, diversification would involve the addition of new industries that are more stable than the existing ones and, more important, that vary in directions opposite to the existing ones.

But greater stability does not necessarily require the addition of new industries. It could involve, for example, simply a diversification of the markets to which the region's existing industries sell. In fact, there are many recent and important cases in which this type of diversification has been achieved by Alberta companies. For example, metering equipment and technology, mobile housing, and heavy equipment, which were previously sold almost exclusively as inputs to the provincial energy sector, are now being widely marked in other areas and for other uses, most of which are not sensitive to shifts in energy investment.[25]

It should be noted in this context that the natural increase in the size and concentration of local markets also adds an important degree of stability to the economy. For example, as recently documented by H. L. Brewer and R. L. Moomaw, regional economic instability definitely decreases with urban size (all other causal factors having been taken into account). This result appears to be related to increases in the diversity of local markets, greater opportunities for import-replacement activities, and the growth of highly stable service activities oriented toward large urban markets.

25. For example, oil and gas metering technology has been adapted for use in urban water systems; the mobile and modular housing designed for use at exploration sites is now being sold around the world; and the heavy equipment and technology developed for the northern transportation needs of the oil and gas industry have been adapted for military and civilian maritime use.

Another dimension of regional economic diversification is the addition of new product lines by existing firms and industries in the region. By expanding the range of commodities produced, firms and industries are able to add stability not only to their own balance sheets but also to the overall regional economy. Examples include the diversification by grain farmers into livestock production, and by some of the large Alberta-based companies (such as ATCO and Nova Corporation of Alberta) into areas like petrochemicals, communications equipment, and miscellaneous manufacturing.

Finally, there is the dimension of diversification emphasized in the Government of Alberta's policy statements; namely, an expansion of activities in the area of raw materials upgrading and processing.[26] On the surface, this may not appear to represent diversification, since it simply involves building upon the province's unstable primary sector. But such activities do contribute to stability in a number of ways. First, the prices and markets for processed commodities generally show significantly less variability than do those for the raw-material inputs, both because of the stabilizing effects of the labor content in value added and because firms producing processed or finished goods often have more control over their markets than do firms producing raw materials (or, as is often the case, greater protection is afforded by governments to finished-goods markets).

Moreover, in many instances, profit margins in the raw-materials end of a business vary in opposite directions to those in the processing end. For example, in 1986, when the upstream component of the Western Canadian oil and gas industry saw a loss of $1.8 billion, the downstream component (refining and marketing) saw its profits almost quadruple to $0.8 billion.[27] In addition, processing activities are generally much more labor intensive than is the primary production upon which they are based. Such upgrading is therefore accompanied by significant employment and population increases in the region, both of which serve to increase the size of local markets. And, as noted above, this, in turn, allows for the expansion of many activities that generate greater stability.

A number of conclusions can be drawn from the foregoing discussion. Perhaps the most important is that, to be effective, a diversification strategy must address all four of the dimensions we have discussed and not focus solely, as is most often the case, on the dimension of adding new industries. Indeed, industrial diversification proper – that is, the addition of new

---

26. See Premier's Policy Statement, *Alberta Hansard*, pp. 3133-3134, and Alberta, *White Paper: Proposals for an Industrial and Science Strategy for Albertans, 1985 to 1990* (Edmonton: Government of Alberta, July 1984).

27. Data from the Petroleum Monitoring Agency, Government of Canada.

industries that not only exhibit less variance than do the existing base industries in the region, but also display negative covariance with them – is likely to be the least practical element of a diversification strategy. It is very difficult to isolate and target new industries that would be economically viable in a region, let alone meet the variance and covariance criteria.

In addition, most of the elements of diversification that we have discussed are really just natural byproducts of regional industrial development. In other words, in tackling the problem of cyclical and random instability, the focus should be on **industrial development** in general rather than on **industrial diversification** per se. Finally, it is clear that an effective diversification strategy need not necessarily involve direct government intervention in the form of targeting specific industries for special incentives, subsidies, and so on. Rather, as demonstrated by the various Alberta examples, much of the market and intra-industry diversification that is needed can be motivated by private self-interest; hence, one important aspect of an effective diversification strategy is its ability to create an environment conducive to these kinds of market-induced diversifications.

Diversification Policies

In general, two basic approaches to regional economic diversification and development can be distinguished. One is the "forced-growth," or "hothouse," approach, where-in one or a few industries (or firms) are targeted for special assistance in the form of capital grants, wage subsidies, loan guarantees, tax expenditures, etc. The other can be referred to as the "shotgun" market-based approach, where-in the objective is to create a favorable environment for development through low taxes, investment in human capital, expenditures on social infrastructure, initiatives to assist in the provision of venture capital, and so on.

In Canada, it is the first approach that has usually been adopted: it is typified by the various programs associated with DREE (Department of Regional Economic Expansion) and its successor, DRIE (Department of Regional and Industrial Expansion). Although this approach has had some important successes, its failures are equally notable and have led to considerable doubt about its overall efficacy. For example, in a recent survey of the numerous studies of regional development policies in Canada, N. H. Lithwick concludes that there is little to show for all of the effort and expenditure.[28] This results, in part, from the fact that, federal governments,

---

28. N. Harvey Lithwick, "Federal Government Regional Economic Development Policies: An Evaluative Survey," in *Disparities and Interregional Adjustment*, research coordinated by Kenneth Norrie (Toronto: University of Toronto Press, 1986).

despite their claims to the contrary, have failed to make a strong or long-term commitment to regional development in Canada. In addition, the limited budgets for this purpose have been primarily allocated to Ontario and Quebec, the most diversified and industrialized regions in Canada. Lithwick also suggests that many, if not most, of the programs initiated by the federal and provincial governments have been unfocused, poorly conceived, and badly implemented.

Many of these problems are most evident in the more spectacular failures, such as the ones documented by Philip Mathias in 1971.[29] Mathias points to the following factors as contributing to such failures: the tendency for regional-development projects to be motivated by politics more than by actual or potential economic viability; the practice of having regions "bid" on projects based on special incentives; the propensity for such incentives to attract poorly qualified or less-than-reputable industrial developers; shortcomings in accounting and accountability, along with the proclivity of governments to accept most of the risk, supply most of the capital, and claim little of the return, even in cases where the venture is highly successful; and, the tendency to focus on short-term job creation rather than long-term development.

As we shall outline later, there are ways of effectively dealing with many of the problems related to this forced-growth approach. But some rather fundamental difficulties nevertheless conspire against its use as the main element of a broadly based diversification strategy. Consider the case in which an incentive is provided to a specific firm that would compete directly, in the same markets, with other existing firms in the region or in other regions. It is easy to see that, in such a situation, the result is both unfair and counter productive. This example alone is sufficient to show the importance of restricting the forced-growth approach to situations in which any such negative spill over impacts are minimal or nonexistent.

The so-called shotgun market-based approach is undoubtedly less attractive from a political standpoint, because the diversification and development resulting from increased expenditures on infrastructure, research, education, etc., are highly diffuse, offering no easily identified industrial monuments that can be directly attributed to a government's diversification policy. Moreover, the approach has certain economic shortcomings. One is that it does not easily allow for the targeting of specific types of development that are especially important for stabilizing the region's economic base. And it does not generally operate on the basis of firm- or activity-specific incentives; an inducement for locating a new activity

29. Philip Mathias, *Forced Growth* (Toronto: James Lorimer and Co., 1971).

in a region would necessarily involve the provision of equivalent incentives to all comparable activities existing in the region.

Thus, not only are the costs to the taxpayer associated with the shotgun approach high, but, in some instances, its effects may amount to little more than a broad, inequitable, and inefficient subsidization of the private sector. In addition, it can be difficult to contain or recoup the benefits of increased expenditures in research and development, human-resource training, and education within the region. Unless there is commensurate growth in the demand for such inputs in the region, the exercise could effectively amount to a subsidization of other regions that are better able to use them productively.

Nonetheless, these shortcomings do not preclude effectiveness in the shotgun market-based approach. On the contrary, many of them can be dealt with through careful program design. Moreover, the approach has the major advantage of allowing market forces to determine the direction of diversifying activities, thereby encouraging economic efficiency. In particular, unlike the forced-growth approach, the shotgun approach does not require governments to select "winners" from among the various types of development (something which they may be ill-equipped to do); it relies on market discipline to ensure that the activities that do not possess long-run viability are allowed to fail, and conversely, that the ones that do are encouraged to expand; and it promotes all of the dimensions of diversification (that is, market diversification, resource upgrading, intrafirm and intra-industry diversification, and industrial diversification), rather than only industrial diversification per se.

It should be apparent from this discussion that an effective diversification and development strategy would generally involve both approaches, as long as each is carefully focused and designed. That is, the shotgun market-based approach should be aimed primarily at correcting market imperfections and creating an overall environment conducive to entrepreneurship and investment. Although some broad targeting might be involved, it would not be focused in large-scale processing or manufacturing activities, as has traditionally been the case in regional diversification and development policies. This point is particularly important, since it is the small businesses in the manufacturing and service sectors that have dominated employment creation in the province in recent years, and since there is no reason to expect this situation to change.

At the same time, however, there must be a strong and growing economic base to support this expansion in the small-business sector, through the generation of export revenues (to pay for the region's substantial imports), the provision of technological spinoffs, and the creation of opportunities for the development of backward and forward linkages. This essentially involves expanding (or creating) "propulsive," or "motor," industries, such as the petrochemical industry, which are characterized by large-scale plants, a dominant export orientation, very capital-intensive production processes, the embodiment of high technology and the use of a highly trained and educated labor force, and extensive backward linkages to existing industries in the region as well as extensive forward linkages that will allow for substantial additional upgrading in the region. To achieve development of the latter type, there is clearly a role for a carefully designed and well-targeted policy based on the forced-growth approach.

Current Provincial Policies

In 1984, the Alberta government released a White Paper entitled Proposals for an Industrial and Science Strategy for Albertans, 1985 to 1990. Its purpose was to promote discussion about the province's industrial policies and the need to reassess policies that had been in place since 1974. In that year Premier Lougheed had set out the following five objectives for Alberta's industrial strategy:

1. to diversify, in the sense of reducing the relative economic importance of the unprocessed-resource sectors;

2. to decentralize economic activity within the province;

3. to promote the growth of the private sector by strengthening small and local businesses;

4. to upgrade the skills of the Alberta work force; and

5. to pursue the competitive advantages available to the province by virtue of its natural resources.

The White Paper's recommendations for the basic objectives of provincial industrial policies differed little in substance from those set out a decade earlier, except, perhaps, for an even greater emphasis on developing the province's human resources and an awareness of economic-development opportunities beyond resource processing.[30]

Although the White Paper came under considerable criticism,[31] it remains one of the few efforts by any provincial government to articulate an industrial strategy. The basic criticisms of the proposals were along much the

---

30. M.L. McMillan, M.B. Percy, and L.S. Wilson, "Proposals for an Industrial and Science Strategy for Albertans, 1985-1990: Innovative or Wishful Thinking?" in *Alberta's Industrial and Science Strategy Proposals*, ed. Michael Walker (Vancouver: Fraser Institute, 1984), p. 28.

31. See Walker, ed., *Alberta's Industrial and Science Strategy Proposals*.

same lines as our critique of diversification strategies in general – namely, they failed to define the precise meaning of diversification and to articulate clearly the rationale for such strategies; they did not address the issue of market failure or of the potential trade-off between the objectives of an industrial policy and real per-capita income raised.

Many of these programs undertaken by the Alberta government are similar to those found in other provinces, especially Ontario and Quebec, and represent, for better or worse, the outcome of interprovincial competition to attract new investments, as well as an effort to promote diversification. What is surprising in reviewing the range of Alberta's programs over time is the modesty of their scope, especially in light of the province's fiscal capacity in the late 1970s. Intervention such as that undertaken in Quebec by the Caisse de Depot du Placement to gain active control of firms was never contemplated as a policy for the Alberta Heritage Savings Trust Fund. Nor was the provincial government's pursuit of industrial firms to open plants in Alberta ever as vigorous or expensive as was the competition among Ontario, Quebec, and various American states for the establishment of new automobile plants in their region.

Many of the diversification initiatives undertaken by the Alberta government are good examples of the shotgun market-based diversification approach described earlier. They are representative of broadly-based diversification – none is dependent on the success of any one or a few projects. Many are focused on creating the infrastructure for development and rely on an element of market discipline. The Alberta government has also used tax policy to promote diversification. The province levies no sales tax and consistently maintains the lowest corporate and personal tax rates, as well as lowest rates of most other indirect taxes, in the country.

Yet these programs, and certainly the tax regime, do little to address directly the economic instability facing the province. Although they attempt to create a more favorable economic climate for investment in the province, these programs are themselves dependent for their funding on the province's fiscal capacity. Hence, the expenditures that are earmarked for the programs tend to fluctuate directly with the revenue position of the government. Similarly, when resource revenues are in decline, the provincial government is forced to increase taxes. The net effect is that the climate for diversification promoted by government policies tends to reflect the very market instability that the programs are designed to offset. The fiscal reforms discussed earlier – a revenue stabilization fund and reform of corporate and personal taxes – would certainly aid the existing package of diversification policies by stabilizing the fiscal capacity of government.

Federal Diversification Policies

Confederation, at least in theory, provides an ideal vehicle for provinces to exploit gains from economic specialization, while relying upon the buffering aspects of the economic union for protection against cyclical fluctuations and secular decline. Yet, in reality, Confederation, as manifested in the policies of the federal government, offers little support to provinces experiencing instability and, at least in the case of Alberta, tends to exacerbate market-based instability. Whalley and Trela note that the risk-pooling component of the economic surplus of Confederation is likely to be small, especially for "have" provinces such as Ontario, Alberta, ar d British Columbia.[32] Inter-regional transfer payments, such as equalization payments, which offset the necessary, efficiency-enhancing market adjustments in "have-not" regions, outweigh the risk-pooling aspects of Confederation. Recent federal programs aimed at the West are often created in reaction to short-term shocks (as in the case of federal aid to the energy and agriculture sectors) and have no longer-term focus. There are, however, exceptions.

In 1987, the federal government announced the creation of the Western Diversification Program (WDP), with a $1.2 billion Western Diversification Fund to be used over a five-year period in the four Western provinces. In addition to providing a new source of funds for the West, this program is intended to help channel the various applications for funding to the federal program best suited to the project in question. The program's mandate is to "top-up" rather than displace other funding sources, and the assistance it offers is in the form of a loan.

To qualify for assistance, a project must be aimed at one or more of the following: the development of new products, the development of new markets, the development of new technologies, the enhancement of productivity, or the replacement of imports from outside Canada.

The actual design of the WDP has many similarities to the range of provincial programs that form Alberta's industrial strategy. The program is broadly based and, like many of industrial programs of the Alberta government, attempts to span industries without picking sectoral winners. It is not clear, however, to what extent the program's expenditures are correcting market failure, as opposed to offsetting realistic market signals regarding the economic viability of the projects. To the extent that it does the former, the initiative is income enhancing in the long-term; to the extent that it does the latter, it serves to reduce national, and perhaps regional, income.

---

32. Whalley and Trela, *Regional Aspects of Confederation*, p. 185.

Costs of Diversification Policies

There are both explicit and implicit costs associated with diversification or industrial-development strategies, and both must be weighed against the expected benefits. The explicit costs are straight-forward, including any direct subsidies, tax expenditures, or artificially high (regulated) product pricing. The implicit costs are much less visible and more easily overlooked. They include such things as negative impacts on other sectors (which arise from the higher taxes required to cover any explicit costs and, more important, any efficiency losses associated with protective tariffs and pricing), and forced growth into areas where the region does not or cannot have a comparative advantage.

In most instances, some version of the "infant industry argument" is used to justify the large explicit and/or implicit costs sometimes associated with diversification or industrial-development initiatives. It is argued that the nurturing and protection of the infant industry will eventually result in a strong and vibrant "adult" industry, which, through the maturity, experience, economies of scale, localization, and urbanization economies achieved, will be able to compete in the absence of protection. Although there are many examples that deny this comforting sequence of events, there are also a fair number that support the argument. With regard to the latter, the Japanese automobile industry is perhaps the classic example. As noted by Michael Cusumano, this industry was nurtured and protected for more than 20 years before it showed signs of becoming the propulsive force that it is today.[33] Indeed, if a similar approach is to be used in diversifying and developing Alberta's economic base, this example can be instructive. The keys to success that it demonstrates include patience, along with a consistent, multidimensional policy approach maintained over a long period of time; the selection of an industry with extensive forward and backward linkages; the folly of expecting multinational firms to adhere to anything but a branch-plant mentality; and the absolute necessity of investing heavily in the development of an indigenous pool of entrepreneurs, managers, and technical experts.

The implicit costs associated with a diversification or industrial-development strategy are potentially much larger than the explicit costs and, accordingly, deserve special attention. The three main elements that will affect the size of the implicit costs are as follows:

1.   The extent to which the strategy focuses on correcting, or compensating for, market imperfections, rather than on attempting to alter fundamental

---

33. Michael A. Cusumano, *The Japanese Automobile Industry* (Cambridge, Mass.: Harvard University Press, 1985).

market forces. In general, it can be argued that, if an industry or activity were truly economically viable in a region, the profit-seeking behavior of free markets would already have established it there. The exception occurs where there are imperfections in the market – imperfections in capital markets that unduly increase the cost, or reduce the availability, of financial capital for new enterprises; imperfections in the information available to entrepreneurs regarding the economics of locating new activities in the region; imperfections associated with the branch-plant approach of large multinational firms; and imperfections arising from agglomeration economies. The latter are associated with a combination of scale, localization, and urbanization economies,[34] and generally form the basis of the "growth-pole" concept in regional development. This concept is perhaps best illustrated by the example of an industrial complex composed of various interrelated activities, each of which, taken singly, would not be economically viable in a region, but which, taken together, create a synergy that makes them so.[35] In any event, it is clear that, to minimize this component of the implicit costs, it is important to focus the diversification or development strategy on correcting legitimate and significant market imperfections and to avoid strategies that go beyond this.

2. The degree to which the policy or strategy impairs normal market adjustments. As noted in Chapter 3, Alberta's better-than-expected economic performance following the collapse of grain and oil prices can be explained in significant part by the rapid and extensive market-driven adjustments that occurred in labor markets and in input costs. Conversely, as argued by many economists,[36] the inability of the Atlantic region to adjust to changing circumstances has been due in large part to policies that have hindered normal market adjustments and served to create a strong dependency on

---

34. Taken together, these economies are referred to as agglomeration economies. The scale economies are internal to the firm and relate solely to the scale of production. Localization economies are external to the firm but internal to the industry; for example, the costs of certain required inputs (such as specialized machinery maintenance and repair) decline as additional firms using the same processes locate in close proximity. Urbanization economies are external to both the firm and the industry, and are related to such things as the lower labor-turnover costs associated with a large, diversified, and trained labor pool concentrated in an urban area.

35. See W. Isard, *Introduction to Regional Science* (New York: Prentice Hall, 1976) for more information on industrial complexes. See also S. Czamanki, *Study of Spatial Industrial Complexes* (Halifax: Dalhousie University, Institute of Public Affairs, 1976) for details pertaining to the formation of these complexes in a Canadian context.

36. See, for example, Courchene, "Avenues of Adjustment"; idem, "The National Energy Program and Fiscal Federation"; idem, "A Market Perspective on Regional Disparities."

subsidies and transfer payments. Hence, if the costs of diversifying and stabilizing a regional economy are to be minimized, it is important to ensure that related policies do not unduly interfere with market-based adjustments.

3.   The extent to which the policy or strategy is aimed at building upon the natural comparative advantages of the region and/or creating new sources of comparative advantage through research and development, high rates of innovation, and so on. It is widely recognized that specialization and trade (along with the division of labor) are key contributors to a high and rising standard of living. Thus, it can be argued that any strategy that implies less specialization based on comparative advantage must involve a cost in the form of lower average (real) per-capita incomes in the region.

While this is no doubt true in a general sense, it does not necessarily mean that extreme specialization is optimal for a region or a nation. For example, just as in the case of a financial portfolio, the present value of a steady income stream can turn out to be higher than that of a variable income stream, even though, on average, the latter is higher. Moreover, it is often difficult to distinguish the areas in which a region has a comparative advantage, since this is neither a simple nor a static concept. For example, comparative advantage can be based on any one, or a combination, of the following: natural resources; cheap labor, taking into account both wage rates and labor efficiency; proximity to markets; agglomeration economies; abundant and high-quality infrastructure; and a highly skilled, entrepreneurial, and adaptable indigenous labor force that is able to achieve rates of innovation exceeding those in other regions.

With regard to rates of innovation, there is also an element of cumulative causation perhaps best illustrated by the Japanese model. That is, in most instances, it is not the degree of access to new technology so much as **the rate of implementation** of new technology that explains technologically based advantages.[37] An initial edge in this area can lead to an expansion in market share, which, in turn, lays the groundwork for more rapid rates of innovation and implementation of technology. This, then, leads to a further gain in the region's advantage, and a further gain in market share.

While it is evident that some of these sources of comparative advantage are based on geographic factors (for example, natural resources or market access) and are therefore not easily changed, others are based on human

---

37. For evidence of this in a Canadian regional context, see Economic Council of Canada, *Living Together: A Study of Regional Disparities* (Ottawa: Supply and Services, 1977), pp. 87-92, and M. Denny and J.D. May, "Intertemporal Changes in Regional Productivity in Canadian Manufacturing," *Canadian Journal of Economics* 14 (1981): 390-408.

factors and can, as such, be altered. In the case of Alberta, it is evident that the main source of natural comparative advantage is based on natural resources. It is much more difficult to determine the areas in which other sources of comparative advantage can be created. Nevertheless, there is an important principle to be followed if the implicit costs associated with a diversification strategy are to be minimized. Specifically, it is that any such strategy should focus only on existing natural comparative advantages and on areas where it can be clearly demonstrated that a long-run comparative advantage based on human factors, rapid rates of implementation of new technology, etc, can be economically and practically created.

A further issue that must be addressed in the context of the costs of diversification strategies is their effect on the economic surplus of Confederation. Provincial industrial strategies often have the effect, whether intentional or otherwise, of promoting import substitution. Efforts to broaden industrial structure or induce the emergence of new industries often take the form of producing goods in the region that were formerly imported either from the rest of Canada or the world. On the one hand, to the extent that provincial industrial strategies correct market failures arising from imperfect labor or capital markets or provide better mechanisms for sharing risk, real incomes in the province, and conceivably in the nation, will rise. Yet, on the other hand, many such policies could further reduce the volume of interregional trade and thereby reduce the gains from the Canadian economic union, or, in other words, dissipate the potential economic surplus of Confederation.

But the costs of these province-building strategies are borne mainly by the province adopting the policies and not by its trading partners. For example, Norrie and Percy assessed the implications for industrial structure and real incomes of a small, resource-based economy such as Alberta using its resource revenues to promote greater industrialization.[38] One strategy that they modelled was the use of resource revenues captured by the provincial government to lower the per-capita tax burden of Alberta residents. Although this strategy led to a significant increase in the relative size of the manufacturing sector and induced growth in aggregate income and population, its net effect (relative to policies in which the provincial government adopted a more neutral mechanism for distributing resource rents to residents) was to reduce per-capita income. Since the costs would be

38. Norrie and Percy, *Energy Price Increases, Economic Rents and Industrial Structure;* idem, "Province-Building and Industrial Structure in a Small, Open Economy," in *Economic Adjustment and Public Policy in Canada: The Second John Deutsch Roundtable on Economic Policy,* ed. Douglas D. Purvis (Kingston: John Deutsch Centre, 1984).

in terms of higher incomes forgone, however, rather than in absolute declines in income, they would not as apparent to residents and policy-makers.

The simulation results also suggested that, during periods of declining resource revenues, this type of policy would induce reductions in aggregate economic activity and offset the incentives for market-based diversification that would normally occur during resource price slumps. The fact that both the low tax profile and level of government expenditures were resource-revenue driven meant that, in the simulations, the fiscal stance of government under such policies was inherently procyclical. Thus, the market component of economic instability was exacerbated by this type of strategy.

Elements of an Effective Diversification/Development Strategy

The foregoing discussion of the dimensions and costs of diversification and the main policy approaches followed to achieve it points to a number of the essential ingredients in an effective diversification or development strategy for Alberta. These are noted below.

Favorable Economic Climate

A major determinant of the success or failure of any new business venture is the overall economic environment as measured by the levels of interest and taxation rates, the rate and stability of growth in incomes and output, movements in the exchange rate, and so on. For the many types of activities that are dependent on local markets, the stability of the regional economy is also critical. While most of these determinants are beyond the control of the provincial government, there are some areas in which its influence can be exerted. First, as noted earlier, much can be accomplished toward stabilizing Alberta's key sectors, as well as the overall provincial economy, through the more aggressive use of countercyclical fiscal policy. Also, by reducing the extent to which oscillations in energy rents are translated into short-term variations in input costs, this can help diminish the market-induced de-diversification (or Dutch Disease) associated with significant upswings in energy prices.

Second, substantial reduction in the variability of the overall provincial economy could be achieved if the perversity of the federal government's approach to its fiscal balances with Alberta were to cease. For example, any significant increases in Alberta's disproportionately small share of federal discretionary spending in areas like procurement and regional development could be extremely important, not just because of the new industry they might bring, but because they would reduce the deflationary impacts of the existing federal tax and expenditure policies in the overall provincial economy.

Policy Focus

There are at least four important dimensions of diversification in the context of cyclical and random instability in a regional economy: industrial diversification involving the addition of industries that exhibit less variability than do those existing in the region and that tend to vary in directions opposite to the existing industries; diversification of the markets for the commodities produced by existing industries; upgrading of primary products in the region prior to their export; and intra-firm and intra-industry diversification involving the expansion of the range of commodities produced by existing firms and industries in the region.

Although there has been a tendency to focus only on the first element, the others are not only more important, but also more attainable. Policy should therefore be aimed at economic development in all its forms, rather than exclusively at industrial diversification per se. Furthermore, in order to minimize the costs and trade-offs associated with a diversification/ development strategy, the following guidelines should be observed:

1. Policies designed to correct significant and legitimate market imperfections should be promoted, and those that go beyond this, avoided. Examples of market imperfections include inadequate information and knowledge regarding investment opportunities in the region; inadequate capital markets, in terms of their inability to pool large amounts of capital for mega-projects and to spread the associated risks; the natural reluctance of traditional capital markets to provide venture capital and to assess the cost and availability of financial capital to a region objectively, on the basis of risk, rather than on the basis of perceptions from a distance concerning the state of confidence in the value of regional assets;[39] the presence of externalities or agglomeration economies that are not or cannot be captured in the profitability calculations of individual entrepreneurs;[40] situations in which non-resident or multinational ownership, combined with the use of non-arms-length valuations and transactions, encourages a branch-plant approach to industrial development, or in which monopoly and/or monopsony are present; and cases where there is a "public goods" element (for example, infrastructure, training and education, research and development, etc.) and hence the market produces less of these than is socially optimal.

---

39. On this point, see Sheila C. Dow, "The Treatment of Money in Regional Economics," *Journal of Regional Science* 27 (1987): 13-24.

40. An example here is the formation of industrial complexes: that is, where the individual components evaluated separately are uneconomical, but taken together, are economical.

2. Policies that unduly interfere with normal market adjustments and that tend
    to create transfer or subsidy dependencies should be avoided.

3. Policies aimed at building upon the natural comparative advantages of the
    region should be promoted, and policies focused on creating new
    comparative advantages should be assessed carefully. The latter should be
    restricted to cases in which it can be clearly demonstrated that a long-run
    comparative advantage based on investment in human capital, rapid rates of
    implementation of new technology, and so on, can be economically and
    practically created. In general, the emphasis should be on expanding rather
    than changing the region's economic base.

Policy Approach

Although there is room for both the shotgun market-based approach and the
traditional approach involving the targeting and subsidization of specific
projects or industries, there are sound economic reasons why a
well-designed version of the former should dominate. One reason is that it is
consistent with broadly-based diversification and development, and its
effects are not determined by the success or failure of one or a few projects.
In addition, it imposes an element of market discipline, thereby encouraging
efficiency; it promotes market-induced diversification in all its forms; and it
is consistent with the diversity of opportunities, across all sectors, for
development and diversification.

It is somewhat more difficult to be unequivocal about the
"forced-growth" approach. In part, this is because it is widely used in other
regions and other countries and, regardless of its imperfections, to suggest
that it not be used in Alberta is tantamount to arguing that the province
should not try to compete for development on equivalent terms. While it
would be preferable, from the perspective of pure theory, for all
regional-development initiatives to be the domain of the federal government,
in order to avoid the problem of regions bidding against one another for
economic development, the fact is that, in Canada, regional development has
evolved as a shared responsibility. More-over, based on the historical record,
it is unlikely that Alberta would fare very well under a system that made
regional development strictly a federal responsibility.

In any case, the objective should be to use this approach selectively and
carefully. That is, its use should generally be limited to projects that:

1. do not represent direct market competition for existing industries in the
    region;

2. have a demonstrable long-run viability, without continued subsidization;

3. are based upon some clear competitive advantage in the form of access to raw materials, access to markets, labor productivity and entrepreneurial skill, innovation, or agglomeration economies; and

4. exhibit strong potential for the use of indigenous labour and the development of extensive backward and/or forward linkages in the region.

There are also a number of important considerations regarding the implementation of this approach. In particular:

1. The targeting and selection of projects for special assistance should be to as great an extent as possible, at arm's length from the political process and should be conducted on the basis of completely independent evaluations undertaken by qualified experts, with the assistance of a blue-ribbon panel of advisers who have extensive business experience. The objective here is to ensure that decisions are based primarily on sound economics rather than on political expediency. In addition, selection at arm's length from the political process should ensure that projects which, due to unforeseeable events, turn out to be non-viable over the long run are allowed to fail rather than be continually propped up for purely political reasons. Moreover, it allows for decisions to be made on the basis of a time horizon that is considerably longer than that associated with the term of political office.

2. There should be an independent audit of each project benefiting from any significant subsidy or tax expenditure. Attention should also be paid to contract terms to ensure that the recipients are accountable and, in the event of an abrogation of the contract, that there is meaningful recourse available to the government or the agency administering the programs. Further, project screening should also include checks concerning the integrity of the proponents, their expertise in relation to the project, and their financial capacity to meet contingencies and to provide for the long-term capital requirements of the project.

3. There should be a mechanism to ensure that programs are closely coordinated with all related and relevant municipal, provincial, and federal policies. The objective here is to avoid the policy and program conflicts that frequently occur and, more importantly to promote the benefits that emerge from the coordination of the various programs in areas such as research and development, procurement, and industrial development.

4. Finally, in both approaches, the primary focus must be on the long term. It takes many years, perhaps even decades, for the significant structural changes promoted by such approaches to become apparent. Thus, two key ingredients for their success will be patience and a long-term, consistent, and sustained effort by all levels of government.

The Privatization Approach

This approach primarily involves the transfer of much of the responsibility for economic stabilization to individuals and firms within the region. In part, this process could involve policies designed to encourage higher private saving rates and lower debt-equity ratios or, more generally, to encourage individuals and firms to adopt behavior more appropriate to a highly variable regional economic environment (such as "preparing for the worst and hoping for the best"). In addition, it might involve the development of schemes that would allow individuals or firms in the most variable sectors to purchase insurance against cyclical and random income instability.

In theory, there is much to recommend policies aimed at encouraging Albertans to adopt behavior more appropriate to a highly variable regional economy. To be realistic, however, it is difficult to alter regional attitudes materially in a world in which memories are often short and in which extrapolative expectations tend to dominate. Moreover, even the most conservatively run households and firms can be quickly swept away in the tidal wave of economic boom and bust. Nevertheless, some aspects of this approach deserve attention. First, even though stabilizing behavior may be difficult to promote, much can be gained by the simple avoidance of policies that encourage destabilizing behavior. As noted earlier, the NEP falls into this latter category: by encouraging many small, Canadian-owned firms to expand rapidly, primarily through debt financing rather than the more traditional method of equity financing, and by basing incentives on holes drilled rather than on reserves discovered, it certainly contributed to the subsequent demise of many of these firms.

Second, there are situations in which the regulatory functions of the provincial and federal governments can be used to encourage stabilizing business practices. Perhaps the best example here is the regulation of regional financial institutions. An important function of these institutions is to bring greater control over financial decision making to the region, as well as greater sensitivity to its particular financial requirements.

Unfortunately, confusion has often surrounded the question of how these objectives can be achieved; in particular, the mistaken belief has prevailed that these objectives dictate that regional financial institutions restrict their lending to activities in the region. Needless to say, recent experience in Alberta points out the folly of such lending practices and clearly indicates that, to be effective, these institutions must be stable. This, in turn, means that their asset base must be diversified, not only across sectors and activities, but also across regions. In any case, changes in regulatory practices aimed at ensuring minimum standards with regard to the quality and diversity of these asset bases can be an important element in stabilizing what remains of this key sector in Alberta.

A potentially significant component of the privatization approach involves the creation of industry or sectoral insurance schemes. In fact, many elements of such an approach to stabilization already exist in agriculture (for example, crop insurance) and, more generally, in the realm of employment (that is, unemployment insurance). In the case of agriculture, this approach would involve the introduction of a more comprehensive system of insurance to allow individual farmers, regardless of whether they specialized in grain or livestock, to buy income stability. That is, by making annual contributions to this fund (perhaps matched by government contributions), farmers would be assured of receiving a certain minimum level of income during periods of cyclical or random adversity.

There are some important advantages to this approach. First, unlike many of the existing types of agricultural assistance, the payments that would be made to farmers under such a scheme would not encourage excessive and destabilizing production levels; that is, the system tends to be more neutral vis-a-vis the market. Second, it allows individual farmers to determine the optimal degree of specialization for their operation, as well as the value that adheres to stability in their particular case. Moreover, if greater stability were desired, farmers would have the opportunity to select the cheaper alternative between intrafarm diversification and income stability insurance. Third, the system would not unduly interfere with the secular or long-run adjustments that are required to maintain an efficient and healthy agricultural sector.

It might also be possible to design a similar system for small oil and gas producers and for small oil-field supply and service firms. These producers and firms are an important element of Alberta's energy sector, but their survival is often threatened by downturns in energy prices, because, unlike the larger companies, they have neither the financial capacity to ride out such fluctuations nor the opportunities to diversify their income sources (for example, by engaging in downstream or other activities). As explained earlier, the response of governments is typically to provide assistance for these small firms, but, in many cases, such assistance results in variations in prices or overall production that serve to undercut the rest of the industry and, ultimately, the provincial public interest. By minimizing these unfavorable spillover effects and by allowing firms to determine for themselves the benefits of stabilization in their particular case, such an insurance scheme could represent a more efficient and effective way of achieving greater stability in this sector.

In summary, the privatization approach should not be viewed as a panacea for Alberta's problem of economic instability. Certain elements of it could, however, represent a useful component in the broad attack that is required. At a minimum, policies that encourage behavior ill-suited to a highly variable regional economic environment should be avoided. In addition, further evaluation to determine the feasibility and practicality of broad insurance schemes for some of the industries most directly affected by cyclical or random swings in resource prices seems warranted.

Summary

The survey results outlined at the beginning of this chapter confirm the seriousness of the instability problem in the eyes of most Albertans. They also indicate a strong desire on the part of the public for policies to deal with it, and a willingness to make sacrifices, if necessary, to achieve greater stability.

As shown by the analyses in previous chapters, the problem cannot be attributed to one major cause. Rather, it arises out of a combination of factors – inappropriate or perverse federal fiscal policies; inadequate or perverse sector-specific stabilization policies; an unstable provincial-government revenue base; and a narrow, resource-dominated economic base. Given this diversity of causes, it is clear that the solution to the problem involves policy changes in a variety of areas and goes well beyond the industrial-diversification solution that is usually touted. The desirable policy changes are examined within four complementary approaches that could contribute to reducing cyclical and random economic instability in Alberta.

Some of the recommendations under each approach are outlined below.

Confederation Approach

- Highly destabilizing sectoral policies such as the NEP should be avoided.

- There should be a reduction in the biases against Alberta in the area of federal fiscal policies or provision of compensating federal fiscal rebates to the province.

- An additional step in the federal budgetary process should be implemented to ensure that the net federal fiscal balance for each province is consistent with its economic conditions, its stabilization requirements and regional fairness.

Provincial Stabilization Approach

- Public infrastructure investment and mega-project investments in the province should be scheduled so they are as consistent as possible with economic stabilization objectives.

- A provincial revenue stabilization fund should be established to compensate for the large variations in resource revenues. This will alow the provincial government to more aggressively pursue an anticyclical fiscal policy.

- Changes to the provincial corporate and personal tax system which would recognize the unusually high degree of income variability in Alberta and allow Albertans to adopt behavior which would reduce this variability should be investigated.

Diversification Approach

- The focus should be on economic development in all of its forms rather than on industrial diversification in the traditional sense. Any policies in this area should be designed to attack legitimate and significant market imperfections and they should not unduly interfere with normal market adjustments. Further, these policies should be restricted to development based on the provinces existing natural comparative advantages and on that where it can be demonstrated that a long-run comparative advantage can realistically be created.

- The dominant element of any diversification/development strategy should be a "shot-gun" market-based approach such as that outlined in the 1984 White Paper.

- Any use of the traditional "forced growth" approach should be limited to ventures which do not represent direct market competition for existing firms in the province, which have demonstrable long-run viability based on a clear comparative advantage and which exhibit strong potential for the development of backward and forwad linkages in the region and the use of indigenous labour and skills.

- Diversification/development programs involving direct government assistance should be administered at arms length or at"almost arms length" from the political process and should involve independent evaluations and audits, the use of a blue-ribbon panel of advisors, and extensive co-ordination with other programs and policies.

Privatization Approach

- Policies should encourage individuals and firms to adopt behavior (with respect to saving rates, debt-equity ratios, etc) more appropriate in a highly variable regional economy. At the very least, policies which encourage destabilizing behavior should be avoided.

- The feasibility and practicality of income insurance schemes for individuals and firms most vulnerable to cyclical or random swings in the process and markets for primary commodities should be investigated.

In conclusion, none of these approaches taken alone represents a panacea for Alberta's very serious problem of economic instability. But taken together – and even if only a modest degree of success is achieved in each – they can dramatically reduce this variability.

6 Conclusions

This study began by noting that the 1980s saw remarkably large swings in economic activity in Alberta. The recession of 1982 lasted longer and was more severe in Alberta than in any other region of the country. The province's slow recovery was aborted by the collapse of energy and agricultural prices in 1986. Surprisingly, the impact on the provincial economy was less dramatic than what many observers predicted in light of the magnitude of the decline in revenues in Alberta's two most basic sectors. Nevertheless, the apparent instability in economic activity increased the public's interest in strategies to stabilize the economy. The conundrum facing policy makers was that, on the one hand, economic specialization was viewed as desirable and as the basis of the provincial economy's ability to generate high incomes and employment, while on the other hand, economic instability, with its associated economic and social disruptions, led many Albertans to demand diversification policies to stabilize the economy. To many observers, industrial diversification was seen as the panacea for the observed economic instability.

Questions relating to the apparent economic instability of the Alberta economy-its causes, consequences, and appropriate policy responses-led us to undertake this research study. We took the approach of posing (and answering) three basic questions regarding the performance of the Alberta economy in the 1980s:

1   What factors account for the severity and length of the province's economic
     downturn in the early 1980s and for its resilience in face of the collapse of
     energy and agricultural prices in 1986?

2.   Is this variability an isolated event specific to the 1980s and attributable to an
     improbable combination of factors that is unlikely to occur again, or is it
     simply the most recent manifestation of an inherent boom-bust cycle?

3.   Given the identified sources of this instability, what are the appropriate
     policy responses?

Our answers to these questions are as follows. First, the economic
downturn in 1982 had its roots in the 1970s and represented, in part, a
predictable market response and adjustment to an unsustainable level of
investment activity. Government policy, however, especially the National
Energy Program, was a major destabilizing factor that accentuated and
prolonged the province's economic difficulties. The better-than-predicted
performance of the Alberta economy in response to the export-price shocks
of 1986 was attributable to a number of factors related to policy and market
adjustments specific to the province's key resource sectors. These include
large reductions in energy taxes and royalties, very significant agricultural
assistance programs, and substantial reductions in production costs,
especially in the energy sector. In addition, the overall fiscal-policy stance
improved, especially with regard to federal policies. But although the fiscal
drag imposed on the Alberta economy by federal revenue and expenditure
policies lessened, its net impact remained negative. Finally, the evidence
indicates that, as a result of market adjustments, provincial policies, and a
variety of factors that have encouraged high levels of entrepreneurship, there
has been progress in the areas of market and intra-industry diversification
and new-industry development.

The evidence with respect to instability indicates that, of all Canada's
regions, Alberta ranks at or near the top. Moreover, the Alberta economy
exhibits significantly more instability than does that of either Oklahoma or
Texas, two U.S. states that share many of Alberta's structural characteristics.
Our analysis of the sources of this instability reveals that, relative to more
stable economies, Alberta's construction sector is particularly unstable, the
variability of employment in all its sectors is very high, and industry
employment tends to vary in opposite directions only in an unusually small
number of cases. Alberta indeed has a serious problem of economic
variability, and this extends back to periods well before the 1980s.

After assessing the public demand for policies to cope with economic
instability, we evaluated four of the main approaches to the problem: the

Confederation, approach in relation to which we emphasized the need for much greater attention to interregional transfers and the effects of the regional distribution of federal fiscal balances; provincial-government stabilization via enhanced countercyclical fiscal policies and sector-specific stabilization schemes; industrial diversification; and policies aimed at encouraging individuals and firms in the province to adopt behavior more consistent with high levels of uncertainty and economic instability.

Our analysis suggests that the policy response to instability should include elements of all four approaches. It is certainly very clear that industrial diversification per se is far from the panacea to the problem of instability that many Albertans believe it to be. The evidence suggests that it is unrealistic to focus exclusively on policies that promote the development of specific industries based on their low variance or negative covariance with those that form the economic base of the province. It would be much more effective, in fact, to adopt a very broad definition of diversification (including diversification of markets and expanded product lines for existing industries, vertical integration, and resource upgrading, along with industrial diversification in the narrower sense), in which the objective is to broaden and expand, rather than to change, the province's economic base. There is also considerable scope for achieving increased stability in the Alberta economy simply by paying more attention to the regional macroeconomic impacts of federal tax and expenditure policies. Similarly, substantial improvements could be achieved if the provincial government broadened and stabilized the tax base of the Alberta government, and if it adopted a more countercyclical fiscal-policy stance. Finally, there is much to be said for avoiding policies that have the effect of encouraging behavior by firms based too heavily on extrapolative expectations and too little on the maximof "preparing for the worst and hoping for the best." Markets are able to deal with risk, and government policies should, where possible, complement rather than counteract market forces. Only where markets clearly fail to reflect the costs of a volatile economy should the burden fall on government to respond.

$\mathbf{A}$ppendices

Appendix A

Net Federal Fiscal Balances by Province, 1961-85

Estimates of federal revenues and expenditures by province are generated by
Statistics Canada (Provincial Economic Accounts, Cat. no. 13-213) using
National Accounts conventions and procedures. These are appropriate for
estimating the regional distribution of national income or output. In several
instances, however, these procedures do not appropriately measure the
regional allocation of federal tax revenues and expenditures for the purpose
of gauging their regional impacts. For example, in the Provincial Economic
Accounts, some federal indirect taxes, such as the Manufacturers Sales Tax,
are allocated on the basis of the location of the producing units. However, for
a small, open economy like Canada's, it is generally argued that these taxes
are primarily borne by consumers. Consequently, they must be re-allocated
on the basis of the location of consumption or on the basis of some weighted
average of consumption and production. Other important adjustments
include a reallocation of interest payments on the federal debt and an
incorporation of the fiscal transfers associated with regulated energy pricing.
The figures for federal fiscal balances provided in the following tables
incorporate all of these required adjustments, using the methodology
outlined in Canada, Department of Finance, "Statement by the Honourable
Donald Macdonald on the Provincial Economic Accounts," press release,
1977, and Whalley and Trela, Regional Aspects of Confederation.

Table A.1
Net Federal Fiscal Balances
(in millions 1987 dollars)

	Nfld.	P.E.I.	N.S.	N.B.	Que.	Ont.	Man.	Sask.	Alta.	B.C.	Terr.	Canada
1961	-312	-106	-959	-513	988	1537	-302	-406	65	29	-140	-1027
1962	-356	-130	-1015	-523	760	1213	-328	-511	13	290	-164	-1662
1963	-337	-141	-996	-519	838	1611	-267	-303	32	376	-172	-864
1964	-311	-141	-956	-484	1336	2769	-142	-185	205	727	-205	1621
1965	-403	-154	-960	-515	1581	3534	-176	-144	328	936	-162	2831
1966	-400	-157	-1089	-560	1320	3164	-288	-177	468	958	-150	1739
1967	-525	-195	-1268	-699	741	3073	-311	-161	517	1014	-151	613
1968	-531	-204	-1403	-705	491	3562	-247	-263	505	1039	-149	933
1969	-605	-220	-1309	-660	1081	5301	-91	-388	778	1668	-146	4257
1970	-649	-228	-1154	-669	271	4454	-256	-642	663	1202	-129	1544
1971	-756	-255	-1277	-827	-593	4647	-409	-757	658	1313	-149	355
1972	-842	-285	-1363	-916	-1184	4632	-385	-835	715	1259	-206	-581
1973	-910	-283	-1418	-969	-564	5451	-422	-656	1491	1880	-150	2211
1974	-1123	-296	-1893	-1145	-1383	5672	-271	-121	4740	1980	-77	4280
1975	-1458	-379	-2519	-1667	-4203	2055	-610	-170	5563	1008	-260	-6859
1976	-1264	-435	-2688	-1741	-3733	1232	-724	1	5305	701	-385	-5390
1977	-1584	-476	-3212	-2007	-6275	-1184	-1186	-337	5940	-99	-465	-12660
1978	-1781	-519	-3252	-2192	-7985	-1905	-1473	-788	5171	-502	-480	-18155
1979	-1648	-467	-3264	-2149	-7876	-2885	-1651	-704	8618	-403	-443	-14818
1980	-1746	-460	-3813	-3002	-10372	-6816	-1915	-223	16612	-848	-508	-15135
1981	-1543	-420	-3497	-2891	-10178	-4464	-1664	-271	17806	-107	-482	-9603
1982	-1949	507	-3475	-2685	-13281	-5788	-2006	-966	11929	-1921	-1274	-24118
1983	-2187	-505	-3585	-2381	-11220	-3996	-2033	-1362	5211	-2308	-1351	-28018
1984	-2266	-584	-3983	-2580	-11223	-4875	-2147	-1484	4262	-3113	-1526	-32202
1985	-2802	-659	-3687	-2592	-10746	-4307	-2213	-1634	2946	-3300	-1577	-33314
Total	-28286	-8207	-54044	-35592	-91408	17688	-21515	-13487	100543	3780	-10903	-184023

Source: Mansell and Schlenker (1988).

Note: Net Federal Fiscal Balance for each region is defined as the sum of all federal revenues collected in the region minus the sum of all federal expenditures in and transfers to the region.

Table A.2
Per Capita Net Federal Fiscal Balances
by Region (1987$)

	Nfld.	P.E.I.	N.S.	N.B.	Que.	Ont.	Man.	Sask.	Alta.	B.C.	Terr.	Canada
1961	-681	-1006	-1301	-857	188	247	-327	-439	49	18	-3686	-56
1962	-760	-1219	-1361	-865	141	191	-350	-550	9	175	-4088	--89
1963	-708	-1310	-1326	-853	153	249	-281	-324	22	221	-4188	-46
1964	-644	-1291	-1266	-793	239	418	-148	-196	144	417	-4875	84
1965	-826	-1412	-1270	-838	278	521	-182	-151	226	521	-3963	144
1966	-811	-1444	-1440	-907	228	454	-299	-186	320	511	-3477	87
1967	-1051	-1786	-1668	-1128	126	431	-323	-169	347	522	-3440	30
1968	-1049	-1855	-1829	-1128	83	490	-255	-274	332	519	-3321	45
1969	-1176	-1985	-1702	-1052	181	718	-93	-405	499	810	-3106	203
1970	-1256	-2074	-1476	-1067	45	590	-261	-683	416	565	-2581	72
1971	-1448	-2276	-1618	-1302	-98	603	-414	-817	404	601	-2814	16
1972	-1589	-2523	-1714	-1432	-196	593	-389	-913	432	562	-3620	-27
1973	-1694	-2480	-1763	-1498	-93	689	-424	-724	882	817	-2499	100
1974	-2072	-2573	-2332	-1751	-226	704	-269	-134	2753	833	-1279	191
1975	-2657	-3243	-3072	-2506	-680	251	-602	-187	3129	414	-4121	-302
1976	-2265	-3687	-3243	-2572	-599	149	-708	1	2886	284	-6018	-234
1977	-2829	-4002	-3856	-2934	-999	-142	-1155	-360	3105	-40	-7158	-544
1978	-3170	-4287	-3881	-3186	-1267	-226	-1427	-835	2608	-198	-2779	-772
1979	-2922	-3826	-3877	-3106	-1243	-339	-1606	-740	4198	-156	-6707	-624
1980	-3084	-3743	-4513	-4320	-1624	-795	-1868	-232	7759	-318	-7585	-629
1981	-2716	-3415	-4129	-4153	-1581	-518	-1622	-280	7960	-39	-6992	-395
1982	-3425	-4124	-4078	-3841	-2050	-664	-1938	-987	5146	-688	-17947	-979
1983	-3796	-4073	-4173	-3368	-1722	-453	-1943	-1373	2214	-817	-19026	-1126
1984	-3907	-4674	-4578	-3618	-1714	-545	-2033	-1475	1814	-1084	-21500	-1282
1985	-4822	-5189	-4190	-3601	-1632	-475	-2070	-1607	1251	-1143	-21313	-1313
Avg.	-2054	-2780	-2626	-2107	-562	126	-839	-562	1956	132	-6903	-298

Source: Mansell and Schlenker (1988).

Table A.3
Net Federal Fiscal Balances (from Table A.2)
Relative to Market Income

	Nfld.	P.E.I.	N.S.	N.B.	Que.	Ont.	Man.	Sask.	Alta.	B.C.	Terr.	Canada
1961	-0.19	-0.28	-0.27	-0.21	0.03	0.03	-0.05	-0.10	0.01	0.00	-0.51	-0.01
1962	-0.21	-0.33	-0.27	-0.20	0.02	0.02	-0.05	-0.09	0.00	0.02	-0.59	-0.01
1963	-0.19	-0.35	-0.26	-0.19	0.02	0.03	-0.04	-0.05	0.00	0.03	-0.60	-0.01
1964	-0.17	-0.31	-0.24	-0.17	0.04	0.05	-0.02	-0.03	0.02	0.05	-0.66	0.01
1965	-0.20	-0.32	-0.23	-0.17	0.04	0.06	-0.03	-0.02	0.03	0.06	-0.52	0.02
1966	-0.19	-0.31	-0.25	-0.17	0.03	0.05	-0.04	-0.03	0.04	0.06	-0.45	0.01
1967	-0.24	-0.39	-0.28	-0.21	0.02	0.04	-0.04	-0.03	0.04	0.06	-0.42	0.00
1968	-0.23	-0.39	-0.29	-0.20	0.01	0.05	-0.03	-0.04	0.04	0.06	-0.39	0.01
1969	-0.24	-0.40	-0.26	-0.18	0.02	0.07	-0.01	-0.06	0.06	0.08	-0.33	0.02
1970	-0.25	-0.38	-0.22	-0.17	0.01	0.05	-0.03	-0.11	0.05	0.06	-0.25	0.01
1971	-0.28	-0.43	-0.23	-0.20	-0.01	0.05	-0.05	-0.11	0.04	0.06	-0.28	0.00
1972	-0.30	-0.44	-0.23	-0.21	-0.02	0.05	-0.04	-0.12	0.04	0.05	-0.36	0.00
1973	-0.29	-0.37	-0.22	-0.21	-0.01	0.05	-0.04	-0.08	0.08	0.07	-0.24	0.01
1974	-0.34	-0.37	-0.29	-0.23	-0.02	0.06	-0.03	-0.01	0.24	0.07	-0.12	0.02
1975	-0.41	-0.48	-0.37	-0.32	-0.07	0.02	-0.06	-0.02	0.26	0.03	-0.36	-0.03
1976	-0.34	-0.49	-0.38	-0.32	-0.05	0.01	-0.07	0.00	0.23	0.02	-0.51	-0.02
1977	-0.41	-0.54	-0.44	-0.36	-0.09	-0.01	-0.11	-0.03	0.25	0.00	-0.55	-0.04
1978	-0.45	-0.54	-0.42	-0.38	-0.11	-0.02	-0.12	-0.08	0.19	-0.01	-0.54	-0.06
1979	-0.39	-0.47	-0.41	-0.36	-0.10	-0.02	-0.14	-0.07	0.29	-0.01	-0.49	-0.05
1980	-0.43	-0.47	-0.49	-0.51	-0.13	-0.06	-0.17	-0.02	0.52	0.02	-0.54	-0.05
1981	-0.36	-0.40	-0.43	-0.47	-0.13	-0.03	-0.13	-0.02	0.49	0.00	-0.47	-0.03
1982	-0.45	-0.49	-0.41	-0.43	-0.17	-0.04	-0.15	-0.08	0.32	0.05	-1.20	-0.07
1983	-0.50	-0.48	-0.42	-0.37	-0.14	-0.03	-0.16	-0.12	0.15	-0.06	-1.28	-0.08
1984	-0.51	-0.52	-0.43	-0.38	-0.14	-0.03	-0.16	-0.13	0.12	-0.08	-1.33	-0.09
1985	-0.61	-0.59	-0.38	-0.37	-0.12	-0.03	-0.15	-0.13	0.08	-0.08	-1.37	-0.09
Avg.	-0.33	-0.42	-0.32	-0.28	-0.04	0.02	-0.08	-0.06	0.14	0.02	-0.57	-0.02

Source: Mansell and Schlenker (1988).

Appendix B
Changes in Employment in Alberta, By Industry
1982-1987 (in thousands)

Industry	1982	1983	1984	1985	1986	1986-1987	1982-1987
1. Agriculture	-11.0	+ 2.7	+ 8.0	- 3.5	+ 2.8	+ 2.5	+1.5
2. Forestry	0.0	n/a	n/a	n/a	n/a	n/a	0.0
3. Mineral Fuels	- 0.5	- 0.7	+ 6.4	- 1.8	+ 3.8	- 1.9	+5.4
4. Services Incidental to Mining	- 4.2	- 1.7	- 2.0	+ 0.3	- 5.3	- 3.4	-16.3
5. Food & Beverages	+ 0.2	- 2.3	- 0.4	+ 1.9	- 1.4	- 1.6	-3.7
6. Rubber, Plastics, Chemicals and Chemical Products	+ 0.1	- 0.5	+ 1.2	- 1.2	+ 0.7	0.0	+0.3
7. Wood Products	- 2.9	+ 0.3	- 0.8	- 0.5	+ 0.3	+ 1.3	-2.2
8. Furniture & Fixtures	+ 0.2	- 0.2	0.0	n/a	n/a	n/a	+0.8
9. Paper and Allied Products	n/a	n/a	n/a	n/a	n/a	n/a	n/a
10. Printing, Publishing, and Allied	- 0.7	- 0.8	+ 0.6	- 2.0	+ 1.8	+ 0.8	-0.3
11. Primary Metal	+ 0.7	- 0.8	- 0.2	+ 1.7	- 0.2	- 1.2	0.0
12. Metal Fabricating	- 3.4	- 0.5	- 0.7	- 1.1	+ 2.3	- 2.2	-5.6
13. Machinery	- 0.4	- 0.8	- 0.8	+ 1.0	- 0.4	- 1.3	-2.8
14. Transportation Equipment	- 0.2	n/a	n/a	n/a	n/a	n/a	0.6
15. Electrical Products	0.0	+ 0.3	+ 0.1	+ 0.9	- 0.8	0.0	+0.4
16. Non-Metallic Mineral Products	- 1.5	- 1.2	- 0.6	+ 0.1	0.0	- 0.4	-3.5
17. Petroleum and Coal products	- 0.8	- 0.8	+ 1.8	- 0.2	- 1.6	+ 1.5	0.0
18. Miscellaneous Manufacturing	+ 0.2	+ 0.2	+ 0.1	- 0.1	- 0.3	0.0	0.0
19 Gen. Contracting	- 1.6	-11.6	- 7.4	- 5.7	+ 3.7	+ 0.5	-22.1
20. Special Trades Contracting	- 8.3	-13.5	-10.3	+ 2.4	- 4.4	+ 5.2	-28.9
21. Transportation	- 4.6	+ 0.3	- 3.5	+ 1.1	- 0.5	- 2.7	- 9.8
22. Storage	n/a	n/a	n/a	n/a	n/a	n/a	n/a
23. Communications	+ 3.6	- 0.1	+ 2.7	- 3.5	+ 0.8	- 0.3	+3.3

Industry	1982	1983	1984	1985	1986	1986-1987	1982-1987
24. Electric, Gas, and Water Utilities	- 0.1	- 0.1	+ 1.2	- 0.2	+ 0.4	- 2.3	-1.1
25. Wholesale Trade	- 2.1	+ 2.0	- 3.8	+ 3.2	- 0.5	- 0.7	-1.9
26. Retail Trade	- 0.2	- 1.3	- 1.8	+ 6.1	+ 9.9	- 4.8	+8.0
27. Finance	+ 1.6	- 0.2	- 1.8	- 0.4	- 1.8	- 0.8	-3.4
28. Insurance Carriers	+ 1.9	- 1.1	+ 1.5	- 1.5	- 0.3	+ 0.1	+0.7
29. Insurance Agencies and Real Estate	+ 4.8	- 5.3	- 2.6	+ 3.3	+ 0.3	+ 0.3	+0.8
30. Education and Related Services	+11.9	+ 5.5	- 4.2	+ 0.7	+ 9.6	+ 4.4	+27.9
31. Health and Welfare Services	- 0.6	+14.1	+ 7.2	- 0.9	+ 1.2	+ 4.3	+25.2
32. Religious Organizations	+ 0.2	+ 0.1	+ 0.5	+ 0.8	- 0.6	+ 0.4	+1.4
33. Amusement and Recreation Svcs.	+ 0.4	+ 3.4	+ 0.1	- 1.6	+ 0.3	+ 2.5	+5.1
34. Services to Business Management	+ 0.7	- 5.4	+ 0.3	+ 1.4	+ 5.7	+ 2.5	+5.1
35. Personal Services	- 1.0	+ 3.9	- 0.3	+ 2.4	+ 2.4	+ 0.1	+7.6
36. Accommodation and Food Services	- 4.2	+ 0.2	+ 3.1	+ 1.0	- 0.4	+ 0.9	+0.6
37. Miscellaneous Services	+ 1.1	- 2.1	+ 0.2	+ 4.3	- 2.2	+ 1.1	+2.3
38. Federal Administration	- 1.5	+ 0.8	+ 1.2	+ 0.6	- 1.5	- 0.1	-0.5
39. Provincial Administration	+ 5.8	- 0.8	- 1.4	+ 2.4	- 1.2	- 1.4	+3.4
40. Municipal Administration	+ 0.3	+ 0.2	+ 1.3	- 0.3	- 1.3	+ 0.9	+1.1

Based on data from special Statistics Canada breakdown for Alberta; Cansim Matricas D775950 to D775974.

Appendix C
Changes in the Markets for Alberta Oil and Gas

Table C.1
Destination of Alberta Deliveries of Oil and Gas,
Selected Years (percentages shown in brackets)

Crude Oil Deliveries to:
(in millions of cubic metres)

Year	Alberta	Other Provinces	U.S.	Total
1976	12.8 (18)	35.0 (49)	23.3 (33)	71.0
1981	15.6 (22)	47.2 (67)	7.2 (10)	70.0
1982	14.1 (21)	44.9 (66)	8.9 (13)	67.9
1983	15.3 (22)	44.4 (62)	10.8 (15)	71.1
1984	17.1 (23)	42.9 (57)	14.8 (20)	74.9
1985	17.1 (23)	37.6 (50)	20.6 (27)	75.6
1986	16.8 (23)	32.6 (44)	24.9 (33)	74.8

Natural Gas Deliveries to:
(in billions of cubic metres)

Year	Alberta	Other Provinces	U.S.	Total
1976	9.6 (17)	24.6 (43)	21.7 (38)	57.8
1981	13.4 (23)	25.7 (43)	18.4 (31)	59.3
1982	14.1 (23)	25.3 (42)	19.9 (33)	60.8
1983	13.7 (24)	24.2 (43)	17.8 (31)	56.8
1984	15.1 (24)	26.8 (43)	19.1 (31)	62.8
1985	15.9 (23)	27.1 (40)	23.2 (34)	67.9
1986	15.1 (24)	27.4 (44)	18.2 (29)	62.6

Source: Alberta Bureau of Statistics, *Alberta Statistical Review*, Second Quarter, 1987 (Tables 46 and 47).

Bibliography

Alberta. *Science and Technology Development in Alberta: A Discussion Paper.* Edmonton: Government of Alberta, 1984.

————. *White Paper: Proposals for an Industrial and Science Strategy for Albertans, 1985 to 1990.* Edmonton: Government of Alberta, July 1984.

Anderson, F.J. *Regional Economic Analysis: A Canadian Perspective.* Toronto: Harcourt Brace Jovanovich, Canada, 1988.

Beaudry, Richard. *Le chomage saisonnier et l'explication des disparites interrigimales de chomage au Canada.* Ottawa: Economic Council of Canada, 1977. Economic Council of Canada Discussion Paper No. 84.

Boadway, Robin, Neil Bruce, and Jack Mintz. "Corporate Taxation in Canada: Towards an Efficient System." In *Tax Policy Options in the 1980s,* ed. Wayne Thirsk and John Whalley. Toronto: Canadian Tax Foundation, 1982.

Brewer, H.L. Measures of Diversification: Predictions of Regional Economic Instability." *Journal of Regional Science* 25 (1985): 463-470.

Brewer, H.L., and Ronald L. Moomaw. "A Note on Population Size, Industrial Diversification and Regional Economic Instability." *Urban Studies* 22 (1985): 349-354.

Canada. Department of Finance. "Statement by the Honourable Donald Macdonald on the Provincial Economic Accounts." Department of Finance Press Release, 1977.

————. Energy, Mines and Resources. *The National Energy Program*. Ottawa: Supply and Services, 1980.

Carmichael, Edward A. *New Stresses on Confederation: Diverging Regional Economies*. Observation no. 28. Toronto: C.D. Howe Institute, 1986.

Conroy, M.E. "Alternative Strategies for Regional Industrial Diversification." *Journal of Regional Science* 14 (1974): 31-46.

————. "The Concept and Measurement of Regional Industrial Diversification." *Southern Economic Journal* 41 (1975): 492-505.

Courchene, Thomas J. "Avenues of Adjustment: The Transfer System and Regional Disparities." In *Canadian Confederation at the Crossroads*, ed. M. Walker, pp. 143-186. Vancouver: Fraser Institute, 1978.

————. "A Market Perspective on Regional Disparities." *Canadian Public Policy* 7 (1981): 506-518.

————. "The National Energy Program and Fiscal Federation: Some Observations." In *Reaction: The National Energy Program*, ed. G.C. Watkins and M.A. Walker. Vancouver: Fraser Institute, 1981.

Cusumano, Michael A. *The Japanese Automobile Industry*. Cambridge, MA: Harvard University Press, 1985.

Czamanski, S. *Study of Spatial Industrial Complexes*. Halifax: Dalhousie University, Institute of Public Affairs, 1976.

DeJong, Edward W. *Economic Diversification and Development for Alberta: A Systematic Approach*. Master's degree project submitted to the Faculty of Environmental Design, University of Calgary, 1984.

Denny, M., and J.D. May. "Intertemporal Changes in Regional Productivity in Canadian Manufacturing." *Canadian Journal of Economics* 14 (1981): 390-408.

Dow, Sheila C. "The Treatment of Money in Regional Economics." *Journal of Regional Science* 27 (1987): 13-24.

Economic Council of Canada. *Living Together: A Study of Regional Disparities*. Ottawa: Supply and Services, 1977.

————. *Financing Confederation*. Ottawa: Supply and Services, 1982.

————. *Western Transition*. Ottawa: Supply and Services, 1984.

Garrison, Charles B., and Albert S. Paulson. "An Entropy Measure of the Geographic Concentration of Economic Activity. *Economic Geography* 49 (1973): 319-324.

Hewings, Geoffrey J.D. *Regional Industrial Analysis and Development.* London: Methuen, 1977.

Innis, Harold. *The Fur Trade in Canada: An Introduction to Canadian Economic History.* Toronto: Oxford University Press, 1927.

———. *The Cod Fisheries: The History of an International Economy.* New Haven, CT: Carnegie Endowment for International Peace, Division of Economics and History, 1940.

Isard, W. *Introduction to Regional Science.* New York: Prentice Hall, 1976.

Jenkins, G.P. "Public Utility Finance and Economic Waste." *Canadian Journal of Economics* 18, (1985): 484-498.

Knudsen, O., and A. Parnes, *Trade Instability and Economic Growth.* Toronto: Lexington Books, 1975.

Kort, John R. "Regional Economic Instability and Industrial Diversification in the U.S." *Land Economics* 57 (1981): 596-608.

Lithwick, N. Harvey. "Federal Government Regional Economic Development Policies: An Evaluative Survey." In *Disparities and Interregional Adjustment,* research coordinated by Kenneth Norrie. Toronto: University of Toronto Press, 1986.

Macintosh, W.A. "Some Aspects of a Pioneer Economy." *Canadian Journal of Economics and Political Science* (1936):457-463.

Macmillan, Katie. *Putting the Cards on the Table: Free Trade and Western Canadian Industries.* Calgary: Canada West Foundation, 1986.

McCormick, P., E.C. Manning, and G. Gibson. *Regional Representation: The Canadian Partnership.* Calgary: Canada West Foundation, 1981.

McMillan, M. L., M.B. Percy, and L.S. Wilson, "Proposals for an Industrial and Science Strategy for Albertans, 1985-1990: Innovative or Wishful Thinking?" In *Alberta's Industrial and Science Strategy Proposals,* ed. Michael Walker. Vancouver: Fraser Institute, 1984.

Mansell, Robert L. *Canadian Regional Inequality: The Process of Adjustment,* Ph.D. dissertation, University of Alberta, 1975.

———. "Texas and Alberta: A Comparison of Regional Economies." *Texas Business Review* 55 (1981): 241-246.

————. "Energy Policy, Prices and Rents: Implications for Regional Growth and Development." In *Still Living Together: Present Trends and Future Directions in Canadian Regional Development,* ed. W.J. Coffey and M. Polese. Montreal: Institute for Research on Public Policy, 1987.

Mansell, Robert L., and Leigh Anderson. "Energy Prices and Economic Growth in Texas." *Review of Regional Economics and Business* 9, no. 2 (1984): 9-18.

Mansell, Robert L., and A.S. Kwaczek. *Model of the Alberta Economy, MAE 2.0.* Project Papers, Vols. 1-10. University of Calgary, 1980.

Mansell, Robert L., and A.S. Kwaczek, and W. Kerr. "An Economic Model of the Alberta Agricultural Sector," *Western Economic Review* 3, no. 4 (1985): 7-24.

Mansell, Robert L., and R. Schlenker. "An Analysis of the Regional Distribution of Federal Fiscal Balances." Working paper, University of Calgary, 1988.

Mathias, Philip. *Forced Growth.* Toronto: James Lorimer, 1971.

Maxwell, J., and C. Pestieau. *Economic Realities of Contemporary Confederation.* Toronto: C.D. Howe Intitute, 1980.

Mills, K.E., M.B. Percy, and L.S. Wilson. "The Influence of Fiscal Incentives on Interregional Migration: Canada, 1961-78." *Canadian Journal of Regional Science* 6 (1983): 207-230.

Mintz, J.M. "An Empirical Estimate of Corporate Tax Refundability and Effective Tax Rates." *Quarterly Journal of Economics* 103 (1988): 225-232).

Mintz, J.M., and Douglas D. Purvis. "Economic Instability: What Is the Appropriate Government Response?" Paper presented at the conference Unstable Commodity Markets: Incomes, Jobs and Public Policy, Calgary, Alberta, April 13-14, 1988.

Norrie, K.H., and M.B. Percy. *Energy Price Increases, Economic Rents and Industrial Structure in a Small Regional Economy.* Economic Council of Canada Discussion Paper no. 201. Ottawa: Economic Council of Canada, 1982.

————. *Economic Rents, Province-Building and Interregional Adjustment: A Two-Region General Equilibrium Analysis.* Economic Council of Canada Discussion Paper no. 230. Ottawa: Economic Council of Canada, 1983.

———. "Province-Building and Industrial Structure in a Small, Open Economy." In *Economic Adjustment and Public Policy in Canada: The Second John Deutsch Roundtable on Economic Policy*, ed. Douglas D. Purvis. Kingston: John Deutsch Centre, 1984.

North, Douglas C. "Location Theory and Regional Economic Growth." *Journal of Political Economy* 62 (1955): 243-258.

Pinchin, H.M. *The Regional Impact of the Canadian Tariff*. Ottawa: Economic Council of Canada, 1979.

Pollock, Richard, and Jack P. Suyderhoud. "The Role of Rainy Day Funds in Achieving Fiscal Stability." *National Tax Journal* 39 (1986): 485-497.

Postner, Harry H., and Lesle M. Wesa. *Employment Instability in Western Canada: A Diversification Analysis of the Manufacturing and Other Sectors*. Economic Council of Canada Discussion Paper no. 275. Ottawa: Economic Council of Canada, 1985.

Richards, John. "The Staple Debates." In *Explorations in Canadian Economic History: Essays in Honour of Irene M. Spry*, ed. Duncan Cameron. Ottawa: University of Ottawa Press, 1985.

Stabler, J.C. "Export and Evolution: The Process of Regional Change." *Land Economics* 44 (1968): 11-23.

Termote, Marc G. "The Growth and Redistribution of the Canadian Population." In *Still Living Together: Recent Trends and Future Directions in Canadian Regional Development*, ed W.J. Coffey and M. Polese. Montreal: Institute for Research on Public Policy, 1987.

Thirlwall, A.P. "Regional Problems Are Balance of Payments Problems." Regional Studies 14 (1980): 419-425.

Tims, David G. "Capital Markets." Unpublished manuscript, Western Centre for Economic Research, Edmonton, 1987.

Walker, Michael, ed. *Alberta's Industrial and Science Strategy Proposals*. Vancouver: Fraser Institute, 1984.

Wasylenko, M.J., and R.A. Erickson. "On Measuring Economic Diversification: Comment." *Land Economics* 54 (1978): 106-110.

Watkins, G.C. "Canadian Oil and Gas Pricing." In *Oil in the Seventies*, ed. G.C. Watkins and M. Walker. Vancouver: Fraser Institute, 1977.

Watkins, M.H. "A Staple Theory of Economic Growth." *Canadian Journal of Economics and Political Science* 29 (1963): 141-158.

Watson, William G. "The Regional Consequences of Free(r) Trade with the United States." In *Still Living Together: Recent Trends and Future Directions in Canadian Regional Development,* ed. W.J. Coffey and M. Polese. Montreal: Institute for Research on Public Policy, 1987.

Whalley, John, and Irene Trela. *Regional Aspects of Confederation.* Royal Commission on the Economic Union and Development Prospects for Canada, vol. 68. Toronto: University of Toronto Press, 1986.

Winer, S.L., and D. Gauthier. *Internal Migration and Fiscal Structure.* Ottawa: Economic Council of Canada, 1982.

Yotopoulos, P.A., and J.B. Nugent. *Economics of Development: Empirical Investigations.* New York: Harper and Row, 1976.

Zuker, R.C., and G.P. Jenkins. *Blue Gold: Hydro-Electric Rent in Canada.* A study prepared for the Economic Council of Canada. Ottawa: Supply and Services, 1984.